# A Spiritual
# Travel Guide
## 2nd Edition

# ISRAEL

# A Spiritual Travel Guide
## 2nd Edition

*A Companion for the
Modern Jewish Pilgrim*

Rabbi Lawrence A. Hoffman

JEWISH LIGHTS Publishing
Woodstock, Vermont

*Israel—A Spiritual Travel Guide, 2nd Edition:*
*A Companion for the Modern Jewish Pilgrim*

2005 Second Printing
2005 First Printing
Copyright © 2005 and 1998 by Lawrence A. Hoffman

Grateful acknowledgment is made for permission to reprint the following materials:

Yehuda Amichai, *Poems of Jerusalem,* New York: Harper & Row, 1996; Lawrence Fine, ed., *Safed Spirituality,* Mahwah, NJ: Paulist Press, 1984; A.D. Gordon, *A.D. Gordon Selected Essays,* North Stratford, NH: Ayer Company, Publishers, Inc., 1938; Danny Siegel, *Before Our Very Eyes: Reading for a Journey Through Israel,* Pittsboro, NC: Town House Press, 1986.

Front cover map: Panoramic Views of the Holy Land by Rabbi H.S. Pinie. Lithography, Turec, 1875. Interior map: Map of the Holy Land by Avraham Bar-Yaakov, 1696. The first Hebrew map of Israel. Both maps courtesy of the National Maritime Museum, Haifa, Israel.

**Library of Congress Cataloging-in-Publication Data**
Available upon request.

First Quality Paperback Original Edition
10 9 8 7 6 5 4 3 2

Manufactured in the United States of America
Cover design by Lindy Gifford
Text design by Chelsea Dippel

Published by Jewish Lights Publishing
A Division of LongHill Partners, Inc.
Sunset Farm Offices, Route 4 / P.O. Box 237
Woodstock, Vermont  05091
Tel.: (802) 457-4000          Fax: (802) 457-4004
www.jewishlights.com

In loving memory of
Rabbi Morris N. Kertzer and Dr. Allen A. Small,
lovers of Israel, the People and the Land.

# Contents

## SECTION TWO

### *T'fillat Haderekh:* **Prayers Before Leaving, for Synagogue and Home**
*or, What to Say on the Eve of Leaving*

## SECTION THREE

### **How to Shape Sacred Time**
*or, How to Prepare While on the Way*

## SECTION FOUR

### **This Place Is Holy**
*or, What to Say at Specific Places*

# Contents

### SECTION FIVE

## The Guide to Blessing
*or, How to Find Blessing Wherever You Go*   **197**

## SECTION SIX

## A Meal in Jerusalem

# *Acknowledgments*

This book has been long in the making, and as such, owes a great deal to very many people. Rabbis Eleanor Smith and Adam Stock Spilker (then still student rabbis) were of help in the preliminary stages of my research. Soon-to-be-rabbi Jennifer Krause continued the research, and Adina Hamik worked with me to get the book ready for production.

Thanks should go to several friends and colleagues who read the manuscript at various stages of its evolution. I received valuable advice from Rabbi Rolando Matalon and Rabbi Shira Milgrom. Rabbi Richard Jacobs, Rabbi Kerry Olitzky, and Rabbi Levi Weiman–Kelman read the manuscript from cover to cover, improving it enormously with their insight, and Adina Hamik took a copy with her to Israel, actually trying it out and offering valuable suggestions based on her experience with it. I also thank Joel Hoffman for supplying the translation of the song, "Jerusalem of Gold."

Stuart Matlins, publisher of Jewish Lights, deserves the abiding thanks of his reading public for making available not just this book, but so many others. Jewish Lights Publishing is more than a business for him; it is his consuming passion, a genuine calling, and an everlasting gift to the world of the spirit. Sandra Korinchak, Arthur Magida, and Jennifer Goneau were exceptional editors, to whom I am grateful.

# L'chayim!
# Eighteen Days of
# Spiritual Preparation

*or*

## What to Do Before You Leave

הִנְנִי מוּכָן וּמְזֻמָּן ...

*Hin'ni mukhan um'zuman . . .*

Here I am, ready and prepared *. . .*

—*Traditional liturgy*

## Something Better
## than "Wow!"

Everyone remembers that first trip to Israel. When I went there my first time, a veteran traveler remarked, "I envy you. You can visit Israel many times, but you can go there the first time only once." Then he added, "Wait and see. Jerusalem really is just a little bit closer to heaven."

Exactly a week later, I was actually there. The first morning, I wandered the Jerusalem streets, amazed at how modern the place was. Turning the corner, I found myself face to face with antiquity. It was the Old City, its walls rising from the ground like a great geological rift of time buckling up through the centuries. I knew instantly what Moses must have felt when he saw the burning bush.

I had felt it the night before too as, in the dark, our taxi climbed the highway to Jerusalem. How many times had I read the old translation of Psalm 24, "Who shall ascend the mountain of the Lord? Who shall stand in His holy place?" How many pilgrims like myself had ascended this very hill through the centuries? At the side of the road, I thought I made out the shapes of rusted tank remains from the 1948 War of Independence, left there purposely, as symbols of the modern-day miracle of the birth of the state.

I would come to know that feeling many times, sometimes in the most unlikely spots, like picnicking with my children in Ashkelon on an old rock that turned out to be part of a genuine Roman column more than 2,000 years old. My kids were unmoved. "Just more ruins," one of them sighed, completely unimpressed by history. We call such people "cultural philistines," I mused. Then I remembered that once, real Philistines sat here, maybe even Goliath himself. Goliath was long gone now, as were the Romans of old, but the Jewish

People and its faith were still here, still alive and well.

Then there was the time I came across the old cemetery in Safed, with the graves of Judaism's brilliant sixteenth-
century mystics. I had sung their songs, read their books,
and knew their names as well as my own, but only then did
their real presence become tangible to me. Or the sunny
afternoon I stood in Jerusalem at King David's grave—
whether he was actually buried there or not, his memory
was freshly felt for sure.

And here was my problem: When I came across such
places, I would just stare in disbelief. All I could find within
me was something approaching "Wow!" Sometimes I'd
clutch my wife's hand or put my arm around my children,
but there was nothing I could say or do to express the religious awe that welled up deep inside my soul.

There must be something better than "Wow!" I
thought. And indeed, there was. I had just never considered
it. It had never occurred to me to look toward the Jewish
tradition for ways to express religious feelings. For my family's stay in Israel I had purchased plane fare, rented an apart-
ment, arranged for the children to attend day camp, and
bought canteens. I had done all the things the guidebooks
tell you to do, but I had not prepared myself spiritually for
the occasion.

Secularism runs so deep that we often reduce spiritual
moments to mere lessons in history. We come to Israel prepared for a detached appreciation of battles and monuments:
how the great King Herod built the Jerusalem walls, or how
sixteenth- and seventeenth-century Ottoman emperors
added to them. We are ready to acknowledge the artistic
side of Israel too. Guides take time out to admire the Cha-
galls in the Knesset or the antiquities at the Israel Museum.
We are good at history, good at aesthetics, not so good at
the life of the spirit.

There must be an easy way for visitors to Israel to do
better than "Wow!" when gripped by the feeling that perhaps we are just a little closer to heaven—or that heaven
has dropped down a little closer to us. This book provides
spiritual preparations for traveling to Israel, and the respons-
es to being there that Jews have practiced since time
immemorial.

It combines ancient blessings with medieval prayers, modern poetry, traditional practices, and the opportunity for spiritual reflection, so you can more deeply appreciate the sacred sites and sounds that make Israel the center of the Jewish world.

This is the book I wish I had had when I went to Israel my first time. It gives you a chance to say more than "Wow!"

To let you take it all in, this introduction has been divided into eighteen short readings: eighteen for *chai*, meaning "life." You have a choice: You may spread them out over three weeks, reading one a night for eighteen nights (excluding Shabbat) or you may read six at a time on each of three *Shabbatot*. Nothing better expresses the spirit of Shabbat than preparing to be a pilgrim to the land of our ancestors. The three-week model is borrowed from ancient rabbinic advice on preparing for Passover. Passover was then a pilgrimage event so grand that the Temple had to triple its staff to handle the sacrifices. Roughly three weeks in advance of the holiday a Torah reading advised Jews to begin their ritual preparation for their journey to Jerusalem.

Think of it: this is the land where Abraham and Sarah established Jewish life 4,000 years ago. It is the very same land where, one thousand years later, David and Solomon established the first Jewish commonwealth; the same land where a second Jewish commonwealth arose about a thousand years later; and the land to which we have come back 2,000 years after that.

Whether you cover one reading a day or six on each Shabbat, the main thing is to take three weeks to go through them all. Do not cram the night before you leave. Do not count on reading whenever you get the chance. Do not squeeze the readings into your crowded day, the way you would a newspaper editorial or junk mail that comes to your home. The operative word is *kavvanah*, the rabbinic term for focusing attention on the spiritual challenge of the moment and not letting your mind wander. Your trip can be just another vacation, or it can be the journey of your life. To make it the latter, do it right. Put aside some sacrosanct time, either five minutes for each of eighteen nights or half an hour on three successive *Shabbatot*.

The Kabbalists began their prayers by saying "*Hin'ni mukhan um'zuman*," "Here I am, ready and prepared." But why both "ready" *and* "prepared"? Why the redundancy? "Ready" means outfitted physically—prayer book in hand, dressed correctly. "Prepared" means outfitted *within*, like an athlete or musician who knows that running shoes and tuned violin strings are only half of what goes into a great performance. The other half is *kavvanah*.

# SET 1

## READING ONE
### *Spiritual Preparation*

Important moments require preparation. Graduations, for instance, do not just happen. The whole school may know that you have completed all the requirements, but you are still expected to list your name with the registrar, pay off all your debts, maybe rent a gown or cap, and sometimes, even attend rehearsal. Your family and friends, meanwhile, need to know the date, and you may need to make hotel reservations for them. The same is true of weddings, or a bar or bat mitzvah; even a birthday party for your ten-year-old. *Everything* takes preparation.

Journeys take preparation too.

Some of the preparation that goes into a trip is mindless detail: picking up the plane tickets or buying the guidebook. Some of it takes thought: where to go and what book to buy. To be sure, it is possible to show up at an airport and ask for a ticket on the next plane to anywhere. But we would look suspiciously at you if you woke up one day and suddenly left town, notifying no one and ignoring whatever schedule you had already set up. Is it possible? Yes. Is it likely? No.

Busy people find it especially difficult to plan their trips the way they like. Some things almost never get done—like buying a book for the airplane, a task likely to be taken care of only in the airport bookstore. But we do take care of necessary *physical* chores, like picking up our tickets or having them mailed to us. And we engage in required *mental* preparation too: deciding how long to stay and who will stay with the kids.

In addition to physical and mental work there is *spiritual* preparation, however, and what we do not do any more is prepare spiritually.

The word "spiritual" scares some people and raises unreal expectations for others. This is not a New Age book; it is a Jewish one. It suggests that you follow no regimen beyond the normal ones that Jewish travelers have traditionally included in their journeys to Israel. They are updated, of course, but they are perfectly consistent with mainstream Jewish practice. Despite the word "spiritual," they are perfectly rational as well, and exactly what you would recommend to your best friends.

There are different kinds of journeys. We go on business trips or we go away "for pleasure." We have obligatory family outings as well as weekend jaunts and day trips to the country. Newspapers herald presidential campaign swings and denounce senatorial junkets to fancy places at taxpayers' expense. Our vocabulary is filled with descriptive terms that set off one kind of trip from another.

The trip you are about to make is properly called a pilgrimage. As outmoded as it sounds, you are about to be a pilgrim to a holy site.

## READING TWO

# *The World Doesn't Really Look Like That*

What does the world look like? Many years ago, I asked my kids that question, and couldn't believe their answer. "The world," they said, "is a tiny ball in space, with clouds that swirl around it. It gets smaller or larger depending on the speed and direction of the space vehicle taking its picture."

That is not the image I received in high school. For me, the world was a double-page map in an atlas, that I later learned was called the Mercator projection. You remember it: a two-dimensional replica of the earth's surface with a crease down the middle that wipes out the eastern fifth of the Atlantic. When you open the atlas, your eye naturally falls on Western Europe, the focus of the right-hand page. My high school classroom sported a globe as well, but no one ever consulted it. We didn't seriously believe that the world looked that way. For the purposes of tests—which was all that mattered—we were expected to memorize the spaces on the atlas version. The world appeared flattened out and elongated at the edges, as if someone had taken a rolling pin to the earth and stretched it into a piece of dough, colored in the countries, scored it vertically and horizontally with lines of latitude and longitude, and baked it solid. It was only a matter of time until someone else took a cookie cutter to the whole thing to make it into a jigsaw puzzle, so kids like me could memorize its shape. No one ever told us that the world doesn't even remotely look like that.

Though it purports to be an objective measure of the world's surface, the Mercator projection was designed as a political instrument for nineteenth-century British colonialism. Mercator was a geographer, but his geography was governed by his nationalism. He made England the center of his map, so that distance away from zero degrees longitude measures distance from the very heart of the British Empire.

Think about it. When you fly across the Atlantic, you do not feel noticeable jolts every time you cross the lines of longitude. The lines are not really there—they are just convenient ways to chart where things are. Lines of latitude are inherently logical, since the equator is the center of the earth relative to the axis around which the earth spins. Distance from the equator really does measure something real: the relationship of a place to the sun, and therefore the relative degree of heat. But distance from zero degrees longitude is arbitrary. There is no center to the earth's surface on the east-west axis—unless, of course, you live in Greenwich.

The Mercator map of the world was colored back

then, mostly with red. Red was used for British colonies, so that glancing at the map was enough to convince you of the far-flung nature of England's holdings. Pity the poor Asians, whose continent was marginal bits of colonial territory at the two edges of the world, not the most populated land mass on earth with such proud and ancient cultures as those of India, Japan, China, and Indonesia.

As someone at *The New Yorker* magazine figured out one day, the world doesn't have to look like that. In what would perhaps be the most famous cartoon ever made, it published an edition with a Saul Steinberg drawing showing what the world looks like according to the map New Yorkers carry around in their own parochial heads: Lots of detail and space for everything east of the Hudson, a little bit of New Jersey across the river, and then some wheat fields, mountains, cacti and palm trees spread out here and there— marking the Plains, the Rockies, and the entire southwest United States.

*The New Yorker* was poking fun at its readership but it illustrated the all-important difference between maps and territory. The actual terrain where we live or travel is our *territory*; *maps* are arbitrary ways we picture it. And, as we shall see, we need more than one picture.

## READING THREE
### *Choosing the Right Map*

Mapmaking is a tricky business, and not always a lighthearted one. In 1967, for instance, after Israel took possession of the West Bank and the Golan Heights, Israeli cartographers redrew maps of Greater Israel, in which the West Bank Arab town of Nablus reappeared as biblical Shechem, the age-old capital of what Prime Minister Begin began calling the territories of Judea and Samaria. *The New York Times* continued to call it Nablus and referred to the territories as "occupied."

A less serious, but equally enlightening instance occurs when people are asked to draw a map of their neighborhood. People who live far from the office take an early train to work and spend little time at home. They draw a simple map with boxes representing their homes and the railroad station, and a criss-cross line standing for the train track that carries them back and forth from their office in the city. To judge by their map, they live in a wasteland miles away from everything else.

COMMUTERS' MAP

Parents who stay home to take care of their children, however, spend large parts of the day in the car driving car pools and keeping the household going. They tend to draw crowded maps with schools, stores, doctors' offices, and friends' houses.

HOUSEHOLDERS' MAP

Children have their own selective perception. Their world is made of relatively empty space with hardly any connective roads joining points of interest. After all, they don't have to figure out how to get anywhere. They just climb into the back seat and climb back out again when new destinations magically appear outside their window. And their destinations are few: home, school, friend's house and candy store!

CHILDREN'S MAP

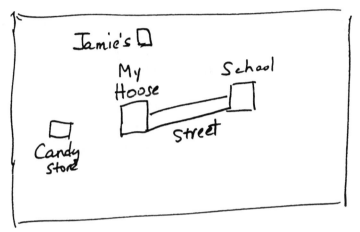

Which map, then, is the right one? The answer is: they all are. New families moving into the suburbs would do well to collect all three maps and allocate them to appropriate family members as they learn their way around town. Commuters find the householders' map confusing. Householders find the commuters' maps inadequate. Maps are properly chosen when they help us accomplish what we want to do. They need not accurately describe the features of the landscapes that exist independently of our needs.

READING FOUR

## A Jewish Map for Jewish Pilgrims

Since maps help us do things, we carry more than one of them inside our heads, and choose the one that will most likely help us do what we have to do. When you open the morning newspapers, you glance at the *weather map* to see what the coming weekend will offer in the way of sunshine. For a brief moment, the world is reduced to a series of weather fronts, its highs and lows enclosed by black lines called isobars that dip down like inverted bell curves into the country's mid-section, and move like sound waves from west to east.

Go on a trip, however, and you buy *road maps* that define the countryside in black and red stripes called highways. *Relief maps* ignore the highways but provide elevation peaks, often in three dimensions so you can actually see how high the mountains are. *Elevation maps* rate hikers' routes as easy, moderate or difficult, and *bicyclers' maps* combine elevation and highway systems to measure how arduous a journey will be.

We are all mapmakers. We all carry around inside our heads a virtual atlas filled with imaginary pages that we consult with regularity as we make our way through the spaces of our lives.

One of the spaces of a Jewish life is *Eretz Yisrael*, the land of Israel. I think I've always known that the Mercator projection was not really *my* map. I am inexorably drawn to the contours of the Jewish map of being, where all roads lead to Jerusalem. I have been praying for Jerusalem all my life. To this day I cry when I hear *Y'rushalayim Shel Zahav* ("Jerusalem of Gold"), the most beautiful song in the world, I sometimes think, composed to celebrate the centrality of Jerusalem. Up north in Israel is the Sea of Galilee, the *Kinneret*, the sea around whose shores my ancestors built the earliest synagogues. It is watered by the Jordan, now a tiny rivulet, but once the mighty waterway where Na'aman the leper bathed under Elisha's watchful eye. Isaiah walked the streets of Tel Aviv, for all I know (even though there was no Tel Aviv yet) and for sure, Elijah's ghost still haunts the caves of Mount Carmel where he once challenged the false prophets of Ba'al. Today, Eged buses roar around the bend as they enter Haifa's harbor. Every time I pass it, I half expect a wizened face with a windswept visage and an arm holding a staff to stop the bus in its tracks: Elijah the prophet, come again.

To the left of where Elijah would be standing, on the Mediterranean side of the highway, your eye encounters the remnant of more modern history: the rusty hulk of an immigrant ship, from which *Ma'pilim*, the émigrés who had fled Hitler's inferno, poured ashore illegally past British blockades.

This is just Jerusalem, the *Galil* (the Galilee), and the Haifa area. I haven't even mentioned the Negev where Abraham and Sarah traveled back and forth in search of water, and which David Ben-Gurion called home; or the mystic alleyways of Safed, where Isaac Luria ushered in Shabbat to the gorgeous poetry his friend had written, a song we sing in synagogue services world over, even now: *L'kha Dodi*.

Forget the Mercator projection. What do I know—or care—about Greenwich, England or lines of longitude or red-blotched colonies? The neural pathways of my brain are engraved with a Jewish map: the map of my life's destiny.

READING FIVE

## The Jewish Map of Jewish Space and Time

I said before that maps are just arbitrary lines joining together dots of one kind or another. What gives a map its character is the feature that is common to all the points. Suppose an infant takes a crayon and scribbles it randomly through the space on a blank piece of paper. You do not get a map. Maps occur when someone intentionally joins together certain points, and *only* certain points, all of which measure something specific: the places where the land meets the sea (you get a map of the coastline) or the sites where many people dwell (you get a map of cities, joined together by highways).

The question for every map is twofold: what *kind* of locations are being joined? And why?

The Jewish map connects places that figure prominently in what we call our sacred history. Some of them are points in the Diaspora: Sura and Pumbedita, the schools just outside Baghdad where rabbis lived and worked in ancient Babylonia; or Auschwitz, the site of evil where so many of our people perished just because they were Jews. Visitors to Spain can relive the Spanish golden age in the old Jewish quarter of Cordova. Prague still houses the sixteenth-century *Altneuschul*, a medieval synagogue that looks like a fortress and boasts a famous external clock where the hands run "backwards" following hour markings in Hebrew letters that obey the rules of Hebrew script and read from left to right, "counterclockwise."

But most of our sacred sites lie inside the territory we now call Israel. Jews have imagined it for centuries, journeying there when they could, picturing it when they couldn't visit.

Once upon a time, and not so long ago, the pictures of Israel were fabrications made up of hints found in sacred scripture. What, after all, could Rashi, our eleventh-century commentator, know of the real shape of *Eretz Yisrael*? He lived before Marco Polo ushered in the age of exploration. Near the end of his life, the Crusaders traveled back and forth from Paris to Jerusalem, but prior to that, Rashi had few people to ask about the land. Still, he yearned to know what it looked like. When he wrote his commentary to the Torah, he drew this map of the land based on what he found in the book of Numbers.

## RASHI'S MAP

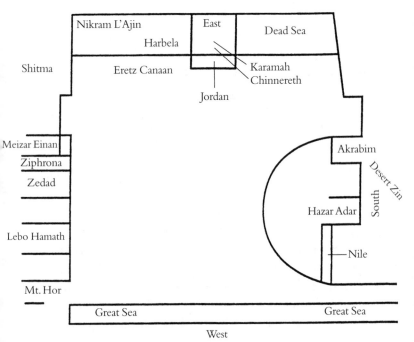

*Source:* Hebrew Maps of the Holy Land *by E. & G. Weintraub, Brüder Hollinek, Wein, 1992.*

On this map, Rashi was thinking in geometric patterns with biblical sites (including the Mediterranean—"The Great Sea") slotted in like boxes. The second-century geographer Ptolemy had already developed the convention by which maps were drawn with north at the top of the page. But by Rashi's time, east went at the top, to indicate the centrality of Jerusalem, city of the East. Since the text says that Israel extends all the way to Egypt, the borders on Rashi's map are the Jordan River on the east; the "Great Sea" on the west; some relatively obscure cities up north; and the Nile, together with the desert, in the south.

In Spain, around the same time, Judah Halevi was writing what became perhaps the most famous poem of a Jew's yearning to revisit the sacred space of our homeland. "My heart is in the East," it began, "but I am in the uttermost West." Legend later recalled that he eventually moved there, only to be trampled to death by a passing Arab horseman as he bent over to kiss the land to which he had been so intensely attached all his life. A thousand years of Jewish readers would memorize the opening stanza of his poem, composed some time before he left Spain: "I am in the west, but my heart is in the east."

## READING SIX
### *Becoming a Jewish Pilgrim*

We Jews still consult the pages of our Jewish atlas, the one our people filled with sacred sites. It is the map we use if we are pilgrims, and if you are reading this book, that is precisely what you are, whether you yet know it or not.

The word "pilgrim" has fallen on hard times. It entered our modern vocabulary through such famous works as Geoffrey Chaucer's *The Canterbury Tales* or John Bunyan's *Pilgrim's Progress*. From Chaucer, we inherited the medieval model of going far from home to get directly in touch with sacred space. Bunyan gave us the pilgrimage of life, a journey from birth to death, with God as our final destination. What the two have in common is the idealized notion of heading for some ultimate, distant, and destined place that is the whole point of being here. America's settlers called themselves "pilgrims" because they thought they were coming to the promised land.

These are not Jewish examples, but change the cast of characters a little, and Jews might easily have composed similar accounts. Western Christian literature depicts pilgrims en route to cures at Lourdes, but Chasidic Jews made similar journeys to their rebbes. When Crusaders conquered Jerusalem in 1099, Christian pilgrims began once again to flock to the land where Jesus had lived and died. But Jews had been making pilgrimage there for 2,000 years. Ever since biblical days, the holidays of Pesach, Sukkot and Shavuot had been expressly designated *r'galim*, from the Hebrew word *regel*, foot, because they were the occasions to travel to Jerusalem and "set foot" there.

As for our lives as sacred journeys, it was Abraham who was first summoned to leave his father's home and "go to the land that I [God] will show you." Both Jacob and Joseph died outside the land of Israel, but they made their heirs promise to bring their bones home for reinterment on sacred soil. We have seen the eleventh-century poet Judah Halevi bemoan the fact that he lived in "the uttermost West" far away from the east where his heart was. But by the twelfth-century, the Crusader routes that brought Christians to Jerusalem opened up Holy Land travel for Jews too. The most famous pilgrim of all, Benjamin of Tudela (twelfth century), traveled for somewhere between five and fourteen years, leaving us a detailed account of Jewish life not only in Israel, but everywhere he went, as far away as present-day Iran.

Pilgrimage is therefore Jewish to the core. Muslims make a *hajj* to Mecca; Christians walk the Via Dolorosa; Hindus bathe in the Ganges; but Jews make pilgrimages also. We have been doing it ever since biblical times.

Some years ago, a sign in New York's Lower East Side announced an organization called the "*Ma'alin B'kodesh Society.*" Its business was transporting the remains of Jews who die in the Diaspora to burial sites in Israel. Even if they made no pilgrimages while alive, they might at least make one after death. *Ma'alin b'kodesh* is the beginning of a talmudic aphorism meaning, "You may add to holiness; you may not decrease it," but the society was using it to mean "going up to holiness." In Jewish geography, moving to Israel is called *aliyah* because *aliyah* means ascending: ascending to greater holiness.

# SET 2

## READING SEVEN
### *Pilgrim or Tourist?*

If life is a pilgrimage, it is also a story with ourselves as the central characters. Teenagers who visit Israel and tell their tale many years after are likely to relate that Israel made them who they were. Those of us who are middle-aged or older go with the sense that the chapters of our lives are being written faster and faster, and that we need to reserve a place for Israel before the plot gets completely written. True, the *Ma'alin B'kodesh Society* will move you to Israel after you die. But even Jews who are marginally religious are likely to wake up one day and know, somehow, that it matters very much that they go to Israel while they are still alive. Their story would be incomplete without it. No wonder tourism is Israel's largest industry.

But tourism is the wrong word for what Jews do when they go to Israel. These are not diversions, these UJA missions, youth-group summers, congregational trips, and bar or bat mitzvah journeys. They are life decisions. Thinking of yourself as a tourist at such a moment wholly misses the point.

For tourism is the ultimate exercise in nothingness. We leave as tourists to "get away from it all." We "do nothing," even "vegetate," or "recharge our batteries," for a successful return to work. Tourists are despised for their garish manners and bloated self-importance. They are dolts armed with cameras, ravaging the very land they visit, trashing it with litter. Tourists are lured by the devious voice of commercial enterprise, which will say anything to attract its trade. They are not pulled by the still small voice of con-science that sends them to Israel because it is time to head home. "For thousands of years," said the old El Al Airlines commercial, "Jews have celebrated Passover with the promise 'Next year in Jerusalem!' Make it *this* year in Jerusalem. Prices have never been lower." Thus Madison Avenue converts the hope for the end of time into a whim for vacation time.

Tourists go to Jerusalem the way they go to Disney-world: not to pray at its sacred Western Wall, but to take pic-tures of other people praying there. They will rearrange the scenery, and even the people, so as to bring back the best picture. I remember vividly one Tisha B'av in Jerusalem. It was dark, but the thousands of flash attachments exploding their light at the old men wailing on the ground lit up the Wall like the Fourth of July. I tried in vain to explain to my children that second only to Yom Kippur, this was the most important fast in all of Judaism; that this is a time of nation-al grief for the destruction of both of our Temples, and the day on which Jews are said to have been expelled from Spain. It looked instead like a movie set or a safari, with hoards of Americans carrying camcorders to catch all the action.

I know, not all tourists are that bad; and not all pilgrims are any better. I am idealizing things somewhat, pushing the two types to their extreme. Thoughtless pilgrims can litter the ground with lunch debris, and honest tourists can respect the lives of the people they visit. But on a spectrum, visitors to a place tend toward one or the other extreme. If they come for enjoyment, a break from the routine before returning home to work, they are tourists—perhaps harmless, perhaps not. Pilgrims come because being in this place is part of who they are, a necessary segment in the story of their lives. If they are on a journey, not to *leave* home, but to *come* home to a deeper place in their soul, then they are pilgrims.

Most Jews visit Israel as pilgrims, not as tourists. At some point, it dawns on them that they are returning home—home to their history, home to their people, home to the place where it all began.

READING EIGHT
## *Sights and Sites*

For tourists, the world is made of "sights"; for pilgrims, it consists of "sites." A "sight" exists only to be seen, whereas a "site" retains its existence even if no one ever sees it. Some things are both, the massive Sinai desert, for example. It is monumental in scope (a sight); but something majestic happened to our people on one of its mountains (making it very much a site).

Sights have universal appeal. You arrive at a sight and cannot take your eyes off it. It is visibly magnificent—the Pacific Redwoods, say, or the Grand Canyon, or even an oddity in nature or in art. It may even be a beautiful surprise—what we call, appropriately enough, "a sight for sore eyes." "What's that funny looking building?" visitors to New York ask about the Flatiron Building, a triangular structure so thin at one end it looks like a stiff wind would blow it over. It is a sight. All you need to appreciate a sight are the eyes with which to see it.

Sites, however, can be so ordinary in appearance as to escape detection. They look pretty much like everything round about them. You have to know about them in advance, usually because you have some connection to them, as when an American asks, "Where is the site of the Battle of Bunker Hill?" Authorities put up "On this site . . ." markers so that visitors can find what they are looking for. We arrive at them committed to their importance, and may, in retrospect, be disappointed at how commonplace they look. We may even go home complaining, "It was so ordinary!"

For Native Americans, the redwoods exemplify a place that is both a sight (the trees are awesome) and a site (the spirits live there; it is home). Some years ago, the federal government licensed the logging industry to drive its daily take of timber through a forest that Native Americans held sacred. The government claimed that the landscape looked exactly like the other areas round about; what difference, then, would a simple road make? But they missed the point, by treating it like a sight. For American Indians, it was a site, the place out of which the tribes had originally sprung, and home now to their ancestors. The government's road was like a two-lane highway through the house where your mother and father had raised you.

Israel is filled with sights. At every turn is something worthy of a perfect picture. It is, after all, a gorgeous land with impeccably blue sky, rocky hills that lead off splendidly into a desert expanse to the south and snowcapped mountains in the north. The wilderness where the Israelites wandered remains as hostile now as it was then. You will know this full well by stopping at the aptly named Dead Sea, the lowest point on earth, where Sodom, the arch-evil city of sin, once stood. But even there, you will find magnificent oases like Ein Gedi, and far away, as the desert ends in the south, the clearest water in the world greets snorkeling visitors at Eilat. If you want sights, Israel will satisfy. But Jews who are pilgrims go for *sites*. We go because what happened there is part of what makes us who we are.

Tourists capture sights in living color. Pilgrims are themselves captured by the site's holiness. They are unexpectedly carried away by what is simultaneously the story of the site and the story of themselves.

We may begin as tourists or even as wary pilgrims in the making, hesitant to trash our Western-style sense of being in control. We may go only marginally invested in the story we are about to experience—certainly not expecting to kiss the Wall, actually pray at someone's tomb, or dip our hands into the soil where Isaac dug his wells and modern day *chalutzim* (pioneers) made the desert bloom. But we may be surprised. The land of Israel may have its own way upon us. We learn to see its sites, not just its sights, to appreciate its enduring sacred character, to know it for what it is: the land toward which we have been heading all our lives.

READING NINE

## *Having a Home*

The desire to return home runs deep in the human spirit. John Denver sold a million records singing, "Country road, take me home, to the place I belong." Home is where the heart is; it is the place they have to let you in; it is the single spot on earth where you can stop running because you are "home free."

And "homing" is human to its core, because most life forms have no permanent home at all. Flowers grow wild; they naturally spread out to protect against being uprooted from a single place and perishing forever. Colorado Aspen trees send root systems underground for miles; common garden mint will take over your own yard and the neighbor's too; Ivy League colleges get their name from a ground cover than attaches to walls and climbs tall buildings to overrun new terrain. Animals at least build makeshift homes, but mostly for their young, or sometimes to establish colonies like beehives and anthills, where strength lies in numbers. But they rarely last beyond the season. When animals more or less return in spring, we grow attached to them precisely because we think they are being human. They become pets when we domesticate them, by making them part of our domiciles, our homes.

Our earliest, but still prehuman, ancestors were no different, but as they grew to be distinctly human they developed real homes. Homes carry memories. We get attached to them. "Homeward bound," Simon and Garfunkel sang. "Home, where my thought's escapin', home where the music's playin', home where my love lies waitin' silently for me." As an earlier ballad had it, "Be it ever so humble, there's no place like home."

The book of Genesis is about a lot of things, but mostly, it is a tale of human beginnings. It therefore strikes an early note on this distinctively human theme of having a home. Of all the creatures God makes, only Adam and Eve receive a home: Eden, the idyllic home we all wish we had. Human tragedy occurs when they are driven from it. The tragedy of homelessness follows regularly thereafter. When Cain kills Abel, he is sentenced to wander the earth: an eternal hunter, not the uniquely human hero of the Bible who settles into landedness. Noah was set adrift, with the entire earth potentially dissolved in endless rain. Thank God for the dove, a divine harbinger of news that land was still left, somewhere, on which, at last, to settle again.

Abraham's father, Terach, has a home, but Abraham is not at home in it. Joseph is sold into bondage to a land not his own, and when he dies, he insists that his brothers at least bury his bones back home when they return. In the meantime, they will suffer the ultimate curse, becoming strangers in a strange land. Only with the Exodus will Jacob's children finally launch their journey home, in a tale that will take the rest of Torah to unfold.

The whole of the Bible, not just the Torah, can fairly be described as a logbook on how we Jews found a home, then lost it in exile, and then returned. Our most famous hero, Moses, is quintessentially in search of a home he never reaches. Like Abraham in his father's house, Moses knows he doesn't belong in the home of his adoptive father, Pharaoh. He escapes to the desert, then is summoned to bring God's people home. He dies looking out across the Jordan at the home he seeks but will never inhabit.

Everything else in the biblical narrative is an extended footnote to this theme of home. Joshua conquers it, the Judges secure it, David and Solomon solidify it, the rest of the kings lose it, Ezra and Nehemiah recover it. The prophets justify its loss and predict (and then celebrate) its return. Deuteronomy sums up all of Jewish history with this single simple paradigm:

> My father was a wandering Aramean. He went down into Egypt to sojourn there. . . . There he became a nation, great, mighty, and numerous. The Egyptians persecuted us . . . and we cried out to God, who listened to us . . . and delivered us. God brought us . . . to the land flowing with milk and honey.

Look at the contrasts! We began as wanderers, but ended as a landed people. Two thousand years of Jewish readers learned that God's greatest gift was a place called home, and in our time, we have returned there.

READING TEN

## *Returning Home*

The curse of homelessness has haunted our People long enough that every schoolchild knows the term, "wandering Jew." The Rabbis encoded this idea early in Jewish thought under the technical designation *galut*, meaning "exile." Since then, we have noisily and stubbornly defined being human as the condition of seeking to be at home, not in exile. Our greatest contribution to the moral standards of humanity is not our discovery of monotheism, but the insistent charge to remember when we had no home. "We were slaves in the land of Egypt," and therefore we insist on a Jewish mandate to end slavery and homelessness for everyone.

Our obsession with home has not necessarily led all of us to settle in our homeland. Even the Rabbis of the Talmud, the very sages who speak unstintingly of exile, lived mostly in Babylonia (modern-day Iraq), and their successors lived in Spain, Italy, Germany, France, or any other land where they were welcomed. Many Jews really did go to live in Israel, of course, but even for those who did not, Israel became a real-life example of where you always knew you belonged. If they didn't move there, they visited; if they couldn't visit, they prayed for it, dreamed of it, and held it softly in their thoughts from far away. For them all, however, Israel was "home."

Not all religions celebrate home-centered geography. Christianity, for instance, successfully became the official religion of the Roman Empire, but at a price: As a global religion, it lost the simplicity of its Jewish home-based origins. Jesus, the Jew, met with his disciples in private homes, and prayed with them as they ate together. Early Christian churches too were homes, not lavish buildings. With the imperialization of Christianity, however, churches became vast imperial chambers and Christian liturgy evolved into pageantry-filled spectacles. Judaism, however, retained its earliest ideal in which homes were so sacred that they had been likened to the Temple.

Every holiday was outfitted with its "home" side: the Passover seder, Shabbat Kiddush, the backyard sukkah,

Chanukah candles, Havdalah, apples and honey on Rosh Hashanah. The synagogue too was outfitted to be a "home" of sorts: a place where wayfarers might spend the night, and where, therefore, home ceremonials like Shabbat Kiddush and candle-lighting became the norm. In Hebrew, the three most common designations for a synagogue are *beit hamidrash*, *beit hat'fillah*, and *beit hak'nesset*, not just a *place* for "study," "prayer" and "gathering," but a *home* (a *bayit*) for these three vital functions.

And when we die, we go again to a home, an eternal one, as Judaism imagines it, ideally, buried in Israel itself.

The master metaphor of "home" is a Jewish gift to the world. Life is the process of heading home to God. Along the way, we have a taste of being with God—the experience of earthly homes where we know we are welcome, where no one hunts us down, where we welcome others the way Abraham did the strangers who arrived at his tent in the heat of the noonday sun.

And to keep all this in the forefront of our consciousness, we visit Israel on occasion: as pilgrims, really going home.

## READING ELEVEN

### *A Pilgrim's Geography: Out of the Wilderness*

Geography matters. It shapes our thinking. In North America, for instance, life on the frontier makes the West wild. Life on the plains brings wind storms, tornadoes, and vastness beyond measure. New York City means concrete and crowding, while "laid-back" Southern California enjoys perpetual sunshine.

But geography is partly what we make it. Jews in *Eretz Yisrael* have been seized by the shape of the land, but the land became what they wanted it to be, through the force of their imagination. Jews in Israel are like Americans in Montana, the Big Sky State. The sky looks bigger there, partly because people who move there imagine it to be so, and therefore, they see it that way. So too, Jerusalem's holiness is partly innate, and partly designed by people who want to make it as sacred as they think it already is.

Most people start their pilgrimage to Israel in Jerusalem these days. They get off the plane at Ben-Gurion Airport and move immediately by car to our sacred center, *Ir Hakodesh* (as we call it), "The Holy City." But that is not how Jews of previous generations arrived there. Before plane travel, they approached it over land or by sea, making Jerusalem the end of the journey not the beginning.

We lose something by starting out where we really ought to end up. Jewish law prohibits shortcuts through sacred places: shortcuts can shortchange us.

Once upon a time, pilgrims got to Jerusalem only after trekking through the wilderness first, not at all unlike the Israelites who journeyed from Egypt.

MAP OF SOUTHERN ISRAEL

South of Jerusalem is the Negev, the Judean desert. Imagine heading endlessly north, and only after many weeks, without watches, calendars, or anyone who had ever gone before you, seeing the capital from the distance. The Negev ends just barely south of the Old City, and is the northernmost extension of the vast Sinai peninsula, where the Israelite ex-slaves first met God. In many ways, 3,000 years haven't changed the terrain very much. You still pass

Bedouin who look like modern-day versions of Abraham, Isaac or Jacob. The sand still swirls in the wind, and heat storms still blow northward into Jerusalem homes. Standing on the limitless desert sand, you can still see an infinity of stars, both of which—sand and stars—God showed Abraham as a sign of how numerous his progeny would some day be.

Just south of Jerusalem, as the road through the Negev starts to climb upward, you still see the caves where the Dead Sea sects lived after leaving Jerusalem because they thought it corrupt—just like New York or Los Angeles in the eyes of some parts of Middle America. You pass the Dead Sea, "the lowest place on earth," says the sign. You will also pass Ein Gedi, where David and his army once hid in cool caves—an oasis, really, where his ancestors watered their flock and dug their wells.

MAP OF NORTHERN ISRAEL

Syria    Golan Heights    Sea of Galilee    Jordan River    Jericho

Mountains of Lebanon          Jezreel Valley          Jerusalem

Other pilgrims, later in time, came from the North, not the South. Before the Babylonian exile (587 B.C.E.), residents north of Jerusalem constituted a separate state that did not recognize Jerusalem as its capital, so they made no pilgrimage to Jerusalem. But some fifty years later, exile ended, and waves of Jews slowly came home. Jerusalem was now the capital for a unified country, and it attracted streams of pilgrim-farmers from up north. After the invasion of Alexander the Great (334 B.C.E.), Israel entered the cultural orbit of

Greece, with ties to Greek-speaking Jews in Asia Minor, the area north of Israel. From there, members of a flourishing Jewish Diaspora would have headed south over the mountains in present-day Lebanon or Syria, and then down the Golan Heights into the Jordan Valley. Following the Jordan south, they too would have come to the city that captured their dreams.

MAP OF EASTERN ISRAEL

Jordan River     Jordanian Plain     Jericho

Jerusalem                               Dead Sea

Jews once came from farther east too. The first-century Jewish historian Josephus reports an unexplained arrival of a band of archers on horseback, who announced, to his surprise, that they were Jews from Babylonia. Whoever these Jews were, they hardly looked Jewish to Josephus. They had followed trade routes from the Tigris-Euphrates valley, through present-day Jordan, and then across the Jordan River into Jerusalem.

From the perspective of Jerusalemites, the Judean desert to the south, the Syrian mountains to the north, and Jordanian plain to the east were all just different degrees of wilderness. Jerusalem was still tiny compared to the great cities where many of these pilgrims had begun their journey, but it was already the Jewish center of gravity, and it has grown, both in grandeur and in significance, ever since.

### READING TWELVE
## A Pilgrim's Geography:
## From the Coastland to the Galil

Another approach to Jerusalem transported pilgrims east-ward from a seaport along the Mediterranean coast. Those of us who fly briefly over it after traveling all night across the Atlantic find it hard to imagine what the "Great Sea" (as the Mediterranean was known) meant to Jews in ancient times. The classical cultures of Greece and Rome grew up along its shores; to a Greek, Morocco was the other end of the world, and the distance from Algiers to Rome was like Moscow to Washington, a far-off capital of a rival empire that shared the world's destiny. As late as the ninth century, Muslims tried to squeeze the life out of Christian Europe by con-trolling the Great Sea's waters. (One Muslim geographer boasted, "The Christians cannot float a plank on it!") It was the life-blood of ancient times.

MAP OF WESTERN ISRAEL

Sea of Galilee    Caesaria    Jaffa    Jerusalem        Ashkelon        Philistines

Mt. Carmel, Haifa

Since there were limits to how much land a pilgrim would willingly traverse, Jews from Italy and North Africa preferred to travel on ships that would dock in Israel's harbors.

These ports were mostly ancient, going back to the Philistines who arrived by ship from Greece about 1200 B.C.E., and included in their midst legendary biblical enemies like Goliath of Gath. With the arrival of Phoenicians up north around Lebanon, and then Greeks and Romans all along the coast, old harbors were enlarged, and new ones sprang up.

The word "Palestine" comes from "Philistine," so perhaps it is appropriate that the Gaza strip, once the stronghold of Philistine culture, is now Palestinian through and through. As you head north from Gaza, however, you reach ancient harbors that are thoroughly Israeli: Jaffa, Caesaria, and Haifa. Jaffa stretches back thirty-six centuries, Haifa thirty-four, Caesaria (only!) twenty-four. Classical empires depended on natural ports to ply their trade, including a regular human cargo of Jewish pilgrims coming from Africa or Europe to holy Israel soil.

The Rabbis were in awe of the Mediterranean. They knew it intimately, partly because they too ran businesses that depended on shipping. Furthermore, after the Romans defeated the Jews and destroyed the Temple in 70 C.E., rabbinic culture was relocated to Yavneh, now a suburb of Tel Aviv, and not far from the port of Jaffa. The sun sets over the Mediterranean by virtually melting into its blue-green water. Our spiritual legacy from those Rabbis still contains a blessing to be said when the Great Sea comes into view.

Over the centuries, one army after another landed its troops on the Mediterranean coast and then proceeded to conquer the land—only to be conquered in turn, as stronger armies arrived later. The Romans took their turn landing here to put down the Jewish rebellion in 70 C.E., and then again, with heavy reinforcements, to fight the Bar Kokhba revolt sixty-five years later. This time, the troops stayed, and a provincial government was set up in the lush farming territory around the *Kinneret,* the Sea of Galilee. The Rabbis followed the government inland, abandoning Yavneh for the area around Tiberias, the main city on the western slope of the sea.

Jews call the Galilee "the Galil." It comprises almost the entire northern part of Israel from the Mediterranean coast, on the east, to the Jordan, on the west. It abuts Lebanon in

the northwest, and Syria in the northeast. It is dominated
by the Sea of Galilee. East of the Jordan is the Transjordan,
now the Kingdom of Jordan and not Israel at all, though
some of the twelve tribes are said to have lived there in biblical days. If you take the Jordan south, the Kingdom of Jordan continues on your left, while on your right, you see the
West Bank. If you take the Jordan north, you pass through
the *Kinneret.* Farther up still, you eventually reach its head
waters in the mountains of Syria, passing through the Golan
Heights.

Jews had settled the entire Galilee during the conquest
of Canaan, then fought for the land under Judges like Deborah who prevailed over the Canaanites in the Jezreel Valley, under the shadow of Mt. Tabor. Later still, the prophet
Elisha had Na'aman, a Syrian general, bathe in the Jordan
in order to be cured of disease. With the Roman relocation,
Jews flocked here again to be near the administrative center
of the country.

Watered by the Jordan, which carried torrents of melt-
ed snow from mountains up north, the area became Israel's
breadbasket. Pilgrims from its cities reached Jerusalem with
relative ease. To this day, the Galil houses most of Israel's
ancient synagogue ruins, a testimonial to its status as the
place where so many people made their home. When
medieval mystics arrived as émigrés after their expulsion
from Spain, they settled in Safed, a mountain community
west of the *Kinneret* (but still in the Galil) adding yet a new

cultural flavor to the centuries-old mix that northern Israel became.

In time, the once prosperous breadbasket became malaria-infested swampland, which twentieth-century immigrants drained to build *kibbutzim*. On the south shore of the *Kinneret*, you can still visit Deganya, the grand-daddy of the *Kibbutz* Movement, started by laborers who were also poets and spiritual visionaries.

As modern-day pilgrims, you will probably spend more time in and around the *Kinneret* than you will in any other area, save Jerusalem itself, the final stop on any pilgrim's itinerary.

# SET 3

## READING THIRTEEN

## *Jerusalem: The Center of the World*

Some 3,000 years ago, Jerusalem was a mountain city of the Jebusites, one of the tribes whom the Israelites encountered when they settled the land. About 1000 B.C.E., King David made it his capital. His son Solomon built the Temple on one of its larger hilly areas, Mt. Zion, whence the name Zion (and later still, Zionist) is derived.

As our holiest city (and holy too to Christianity and Islam), there are more legends about Jerusalem than about any other city in Western history, maybe in the world. The midrash hints at its mythic richness when it says that Jerusalem has seventy names, including *Shalom,* "Peace"; *Marom,* "Heights"; *M'nuchah,* "Rest"; *Yafeh,* "Beautiful"; *Y'didut,* "Beloved"; *M'tsudah,* "Fortress"; *Gilah,* "Joy"; *Gan Adonai,* "Garden of God"; *Ir Hayonah,* "City of Doves"; *Kiryah Ne'emanah,* "Faithful City"; *Ir Hatzedek,* "City of Righteousness"; *Gei Chizayon,* "Valley of Vision," *Daltot Ha'amim,* "Doorway for the World's Peoples"; and even *Eden,* the garden of gardens itself.

Today's Jerusalem features flowers everywhere; gardeners

Babylonian Exile · · · · Ezekiel in Babylonia · · · ·

King Josiah/Deuteronomy

587 B.C.E.

621 B.C.E.

King David builds Jerusalem

C. 1000 B.C.E.

learned to water them one by one when this was still the upward region of the Judean desert, and Jerusalemites never kept the tap running because water was so scarce.

In its relationship to our people, Jerusalem is most frequently likened to a mother. She is sometimes thought of also as a young unmarried woman, *b'tulah*, or a bride, *kallah*, and even a barren woman, *akarah*, bereft of her children who languish in exile. She mourns their absence while patiently awaiting their return.

Though David had settled Jerusalem by the tenth century, it took three centuries more for it to emerge as Israel's only sacred center. In 621 B.C.E., King Josiah announced that he had discovered an age-old sacred book (the book of Deuteronomy) demanding that sacrifices be offered only in Jerusalem. Rival shrines in northern sites were successfully rooted out, and from that day onward, no other city has challenged Jerusalem's hegemony in Jewish imagination.

About a century later, the prophet Ezekiel envisioned Jerusalem from his place of exile in Babylonia, calling it, for the first time, God's holy mountain. His idealized geometry placed it literally in the geographic center of the country, leading rabbinic tradition to imagine all of Israel as a set of concentric circles, like ripples of the sacred, emanating outward from the Holy of Holies within the Temple precinct. The Temple disappeared, pummeled into dust by Roman battering rams. The ripples of this destruction continue through time.

The Romans left standing only a single external structure to the west that had been used as a retaining wall for the Temple's foundation. Known as the "Western Wall" and even the "Wailing Wall," Jews now call it simply "the Wall" (in Hebrew, "the *Kotel*"). High above the Wall sits the site where the Temple once stood. It is the most sacred place we know. The axis of the earth is there, the Rabbis said. From there peace will be announced to all the world. No matter how you arrive, it is still the holy mountain, Jerusalem of Gold, the Garden of Eden, and mother to Jews the world over.

READING FOURTEEN

## *Where You Know that You Feel What You Cannot See*

Think of Israel the way pilgrims always have:

- Jerusalem in the center.
- A desert wilderness to the south, where Abraham and Sarah camped, and where Egyptian slaves first made their appearance on their memorable return home.
- A mountain run to the north, still visible from the Galil, and approachable in the foothills called the Golan Heights; it is in the Galil where life went on in farms and mountain towns, from Roman times until our own.
- A coastal plain westward in luscious proximity to the Great Sea. Here lay the commercial hub that connects Israel to civilizations whose ships have docked with ideas and with goods for centuries.
- To the east lay empires that changed hands with every passing century: first Babylonia, then Persia, then Babylonia again, then various Muslim dynasties. It didn't matter. Jews came from one empire or another with equal fervor, crossing the Jordan eventually, passing through Bethlehem perhaps (hence the Christian story of the inn that had no room for Jesus), and then climbing to Jerusalem with the rising sun at their back, so that when they got to the city of their dreams, they saw it sparkling and alive with the brilliant play of golds and yellows.

You will get the history of all these places. Israeli guides are good at that. And you cannot miss the beauty of the landscape. God is good at that! You will not easily miss the pulse of modern life alongside echoes of antiquity in this country that survives history even as it remembers it. What you can so easily miss is a sense of the sacred, without which all of this is just another pretty place with ruins, one more set of things to see before moving on to next year's tourist finds.

Throughout the world, the sacred evokes ritual: bathing in the Ganges; spirit quests in Native American forests; and inserting notes of prayer in the crevices of the *Kotel*. Why not? Should space be any different from time? Whether we notice or not, Shabbat falls every seven days. But because we *want* to notice, we adopt ritual welcomes and farewells as Shabbat comes and goes. Without Kiddush and candles Shabbat steals in too silently to attract attention; without Havdalah, it steals away with equal ease. So too, Yom Kippur or Pesach give us telltale signs of *Kol Nidrei* and seder tunes. Even secular time demands some ritual attention: watching the ball drop on New Year's Eve or blowing out the candles on a birthday cake.

So too with secular space: A visitor to the United States House of Representatives describes being invited by a friendly insider to mount the speaker's podium late one night when no one was in the chamber. "Not a chance," he replied, "It felt like the *bimah* in my synagogue. I couldn't go up there without a blessing, or something." That is exactly how sensitive visitors feel when they walk through the Jaffa Gate into the Old City of Jerusalem or stand on the street where Isaiah walked. "There ought to be a blessing, or something."

There usually is a "blessing, or something." Moses took off his shoes when he saw the burning bush. He might equally well have passed it by with a simple "very interesting," or even whatever word he used for "Wow!" Blessed with cameras, as he was not, we are more likely to settle for a picture. But as we shall see, a picture is not enough. Cameras reproduce the horizon but they cannot show what they cannot see. This book encourages you to get in touch with the dimensions of experience that cannot be seen.

READING FIFTEEN

# What I Learned from My Grandfather's Watch

My grandfather taught me to tell time. He worked his whole life for almost nothing. Yet each night he managed to bring home his prized possession: a railroad watch that sparkled in the sun when he let it dangle out of the pocket where it lodged. I used to stare at it from the comfort of his lap.

There was a certain magic about the way he said it worked. Just three hands of different sizes that somehow measured time in hours, minutes, and even seconds.

Years later, I graduated to modern Casio watches that flashed the time more accurately in single digital readouts, and I learned the difference between digital and analog displays. Mercury thermometers, old-time bathroom scales, and railroad watches are analog. They provide a spatial analogy to the flow of time, weight or temperature; as time passes, pounds increase, or temperature rises, an arbitrary marker (hands on a clock, numbers on a scale, and the mercury level in the thermometer) move through a space that is calibrated roughly to correspond to the thing being measured. You can watch time fly, weight change, and temperature alter by keeping your eyes glued to the watch hand, the scale dial, or the thermometer gauge.

But analog indicators are approximate. Computers provide more exact digital readouts. Your watch says 9:42 until, exactly one minute later, it skips to 9:43. The room registers at exactly 87 degrees Fahrenheit. The scale lights up at a precise weight of 107.5 pounds.

Something within us loves precision. We prefer digital measurements even though the world doesn't really work that way. Time does not jolt forward second by second, and both temperature and weight build up slowly. We just like the idea of exactitude. So we pretend that we can arrest changing speed or time or anything else in mid-movement, holding it there until the next precise measurement is reached.

That is the kind of thinking that goes into the formation of religious celebration. We like to know *exactly* when

Shabbat begins, a holiday ends, or services commence. Countless brides and grooms have asked their rabbi, "Exactly when in the ceremony do we actually become married?" Secular celebration works the same way. Wanting to know the exact time to ring in the new year, we count down to it, and then erupt with "Happy New Year." Ritual converts the natural flow of time, which is analogic, into the arbitrary, make-believe time of digital precision, by imagining an exact stoppage of time at which an event takes place.

Human celebration, religious or secular, thus requires that we imagine an arbitrary time at which the thing in question is said to occur: the second we really turn twenty-one, the moment of actual sunrise, the time when day magically becomes night. For some time prior, we learn to *anticipate* it—the month of Elul that precedes Rosh Hashanah, the three-week set of Torah readings in synagogue that warn us of Passover's imminent arrival, or the six-week hype before a superbowl. Then just before it arrives, we frenetically increase our attention to the event as we watch it *approach*—getting ready for Rosh Hashanah dinner, cleaning house for the Seder, or preparing the Superbowl party.

And then it arrives: Kiddush with apples and honey, the first page of the Haggadah, or the kick-off for the big game. In all three cases, *anticipation* and then *approach* culminate in ritual *acknowledgment*. We savor the moment only if we have taken requisite care to build up to it, and then to be ready to mark it when it comes.

And if we are successful, we keep the moment alive for a while afterward. With happy events, we speak of an afterglow. But even sad occasions last beyond the moment of ritual closure—a funeral, for instance, provides memories that affect us profoundly for years to come. As much as we have to take care to build up to the moments that matter, we need to nurture the echoes of their occurrence in the recesses of our memories.

READING SIXTEEN

# Anticipate, Approach, Acknowledge— and Afterthought

Modern clocks were not invented until the thirteenth or fourteenth century. Until then, people used the equivalent of hourglasses with the flow of water or sand to mark the passing of time. No one ever knew exactly what time it was. Things began when they began and lasted as long as they lasted. Now, by contrast, we are conditioned to move from one thing to another, barely recalling the one we finish, allotting no time to get ready for the one approaching. It's called efficiency.

Matters of the heart and of the spirit, however, cannot be squeezed into a convenient time slot and then quickly put on hold. They require anticipation and approach before they can be acknowledged. They need to be replayed in our memories afterward; otherwise, we rob ourselves of the full depth of these events that mark time's passing. We rob our heirs as well: our children and grandchildren will never know what we have learned if we do not take time to savor it ourselves—and then record it for them.

Traditional ritual compensates for the rush that permeates modern life. It makes us stretch the single moment of the "happening" by preparation and afterthought. It prevents us from exhausting all our energy on a single fleeting moment without attending to the rules and regulations that come before and after. Birthdays, for example, are anticipated by months of sending invitations and planning the party. They are then approached by a day of excitement as last feverish preparations are made (even though the person with the birthday and the family pretend to each other that nothing is going to happen). The birthday highlight (blowing out the candles on the cake) is followed by singing "Happy Birthday," and then cutting and eating the cake—as often as not a poorly made commercial one that no one wants anyway, but which everyone eats anyhow, rather than rudely cutting the ritual short and just going home.

What goes for birthdays, goes for other rituals too. People anticipate New Year's Eve by making dates and reservations in November or December, even to the point of transforming excitement into anxiety. Then they approach the digital moment by watching the ball slowly descend from the tower in Times Square, so that when it does, they can stop the motion magically and enjoy the precise instant when the new year comes into being. But the night is still young. The band keeps playing; the party continues for hours; and there is still New Year's Day, with football games, parties to attend, and a feel of the new year to share with neighbors.

We appreciate the digital moments of ritual only if we pay attention to the preceding build-up of anticipation and approach. Otherwise the moments that matter arrive unheralded. Similarly, those moments matter more if we bask in their glory after they have occurred, and record them before they escape into forgetfulness.

You will appreciate the sacred sites of your pilgrimage if you prepare for them first and let them linger for a while afterward. The magic recipe is therefore, "Anticipate, Approach, Acknowledge, Afterthought."

The night before, *anticipate* what you are going to see.

As you get there the next day, *approach* the site with all the expectation you can muster, as if it is the only spot on earth that matters.

When you finally arrive, *acknowledge* its sacred presence.

After you leave, record your *afterthoughts* about what you experienced.

This book has arranged each site with these requirements in mind.

First, you are given a reading to *anticipate* where you are going. Read it at the end of the preceding day, then go to bed with one of its phrases ringing in your ears.

You then will find another reading for the next day. Use it for the ride or walk to the place in question. It allows you to *approach* the site with nothing else on your mind. Often it is a psalm or a prayer that pilgrims have used to approach this place for centuries.

When you finally arrive, you get a third reading, usually a blessing. Blessings are the Jewish route to the sacred. Say the blessing to *acknowledge* being there, and drink in the magic of the place. Let it become part of your being.

Then later on still, record your *afterthoughts*—for your-self and for posterity.

## READING SEVENTEEN
### *Blessings!*

Mostly, this is a book of blessings. Blessings are a brilliant mode of spiritual expression designed by the Rabbis some 2,000 years ago. They are now so integral to Jewish spirituality that they are taken for granted, even though they are the key to Judaism's uniqueness.

The Rabbis followed the psalmist's view that "The earth is God's and the fullness thereof, the world and they that dwell therein." God is therefore everywhere, apt to break in upon us at any moment—in the fullness of a spring blossom, the raw force of a thunderstorm or a memory in the march of time. Rather than let such moments pass unrecognized, the Rabbis outfitted Judaism with blessings, a simple but eloquent genre of appreciation for life's special moments.

Blessings are immediately recognizable by their form. You probably know some of them by heart but have never considered how unique to Judaism they are, and with what genius they were invented. They are usually one-liners that recur so frequently in Jewish prayers that most Jews memorize their opening formula without even meaning to:

בָּרוּךְ אַתָּה יְיָ אֱלֹהֵינוּ מֶלֶךְ הָעוֹלָם ....

*Barukh atah Adonai Eloheinu melekh ha'olam ....*

The usual word-for-word translation is, "Blessed art thou, Lord our God, King of the Universe. . . ." But it is often shortened to "Blessed is God. . . ." That is the way it appears in this book. Either way, the idea is that at moments that matter, we pause to acknowledge the presence of God.

That simple introductory formula is expanded to encompass the particular event we have in mind. We begin a meal, for instance, only after acknowledging God's gift of food in the first place (and, implicitly, the Rabbis say, by praying for food in abundance, some day, for all the world's hungry people).

בָּרוּךְ אַתָּה יְיָ אֱלֹהֵינוּ מֶלֶךְ הָעוֹלָם
הַמּוֹצִיא לֶחֶם מִן הָאָרֶץ.

*Barukh atah Adonai, Eloheinu melekh ha'olam, hamotsi lechem min ha'aretz.*

**Blessed is God, who brings forth bread from the earth.**

Similarly, when encountering a place where a miracle of history once occurred—maybe you should memorize this one; you will be using it a lot—we say:

בָּרוּךְ אַתָּה יְיָ אֱלֹהֵינוּ מֶלֶךְ הָעוֹלָם
שֶׁעָשָׂה נִסִּים לַאֲבוֹתֵינוּ בַּמָּקוֹם הַזֶּה.

*Barukh atah Adonai, Eloheinu melekh ha'olam, she'asah nissim la'avoteinu bamakom hazeh.*

**Blessed is God, who performed miracles for our ancestors in this very place.**

When Israel's poet laureate S.Y. Agnon went to Copenhagen to receive the Nobel Prize for literature, observers were surprised to find him conversing briefly with the Swedish monarch who presented him with the award. Careful rehearsal had impressed on the recipients the need to retain the strict formality of courtroom etiquette, whereby they were simply to march down the aisle, take the award, bow, and leave.

When questioned as to what he had said, Agnon explained, "I am a Jew. I have inherited many blessings from my ancestors, including one to be said in the presence of royalty. But I have never stood before a king or queen. Finally I got to say a blessing that has eluded me all these years, 'Blessed is God, who shares divine glory with earthly rulers.'"

Not all of us can be poets laureate or recipients of the Nobel Prize. But we all share Agnon's heritage of blessings, and visiting Israel gives us a chance to greet Israel's marvels with the same age-old formulas as Agnon drew upon to greet a modern-day monarch.

The most important part of this book is its blessings, a chance to get in touch with the sacred in an authentically Jewish way, inherited from 2,000 years of history. Reaching deep down into the collective memory of the Jewish people to find a genuine spiritual response to the sites of our ancient land is better than saying a simple, modern, succinct "Wow."

## READING EIGHTEEN
# *A Pilgrim's Diary: Memories in the Making*

Another Nobel Prize winner for literature, Isaac Bashevis Singer, is reputed to have said, "We Jews have many faults, but amnesia is not among them." A visit to Israel will convince you of the Jewish persistence of memory. We may be the people of the book, but our book of books is a record of what we choose to remember. Long before Americans were remembering the Alamo, we were taught to remember that we had been slaves in the land of Egypt. We light *yahrzeit* (memorial) candles to remember those who die. We say *Yizkor*, our memorial service, several times a year, and on Rosh Hashanah, we ask God, "Remember us for life."

Part of being made in God's image is this gift of memory. It is not clear, for instance, how much other forms of life can even do this. Beyond their inherited instincts, imprinted in their genetic code from millions of years of evolution, animals remember relatively little. Try training your pet dog to do a simple trick. You need a great deal of positive reinforcement. By contrast, humans revel in memory work. The reason is simple. We are, above all, meaning-making animals. And memory is how we find patterns from the past that make life meaningful.

The world strikes our senses, and we are immediately driven to interpret it: not simply for practical ends—animals do that too, deciding if this sound or that shadow means danger or opportunity—but as artistic constructs. Forest animals can analyze the shape of cloud formations to see if a storm is imminent; only human beings expect that the clouds will also reveal patterns, beauty, and design.

From the perspective of animals, the land of Israel is just so much sand, rock, and sunshine. For human beings, it can be much more. For Jews, it is more still. It is a land where our people met God, and where we hope to do the same.

A pilgrimage is an exercise in stretching your memory. If you emerge from the experience richer for it, it will be because you have become more richly human by being more fully Jewish. That is the point of the *Afterthought* section provided for each of the sites covered in this book.

To get the most from your journey, take the time and effort to sustain your capacity for memory. You will be adding your memories to those of the countless generations who came before you. As you stand on ancient ruins, or see the sun over the Mediterranean, or eat in a settlement where once there was only malarial swamp, you may find a million thoughts and emotions coursing through you. You will take pictures to savor the moment, as you should, but do not ask the pictures to do more than they can. They can make two-dimensional copies of three-dimensional experiences, but they can never reproduce what you felt at that moment, what you said in your heart you would always remember, what you promised to tell your children or grandchildren someday.

The essence of the spiritual life is keeping alive the deep-seated thoughts and feelings that rise to consciousness at such moments. If you let them slip away, they may never return. So write them down. Memory is partly what you draw from your past and partly what generations yet to come will inherit from you. Do your bit to sustain memory beyond yourself. Make your experience part of the Jewish People's heritage.

In the end, this is more than a guidebook. It is a pilgrim's diary, and you are the pilgrim. Enter your response to the sites you visit as memories in the making, and you will have them forever: for you and for those you love, this will be *your* contribution to the memory of this people that has never suffered from amnesia.

# T'fillat Haderekh:
# Prayers Before Leaving,
# for Synagogue and Home

*or*

*What to Say on the Eve of Leaving*

I rejoiced when they said to me,
"Let us go to the house of God."

—*Psalm 122:1*

# For the Shabbat Prior to Leaving

## A Prayer for the Shabbat Table

Those leaving on pilgrimage to Israel during the week to come should recite the following, if possible, in the company of friends and family who are invited to share the moment of anticipation around the Shabbat table.

> May the One who blessed our ancestors,
>     Abraham, Isaac, and Jacob,
>     Sarah, Rebekah, Rachel and Leah,
> Bless me and those with whom I travel,
> On this, our journey up to Israel.
> May we travel safely,
> And arrive in peace to the land that we hold dear,
>     the land that we call Zion.
> May we return to those we love
>     blessed in every undertaking
>     inspired and renewed by our People in our land.
> Amen.

It is customary to collect written prayers to insert into the *Kotel*, the Wall, and token amounts of *tz'dakah* (charity) to leave with the poor in Israel (the usual amount is a dollar, but some give more). Explain to those around the table that you are happy to take any prayers that they write out and monetary gifts they leave with you. The former will be deposited in the cracks of the Wall, and the latter will be dispersed at your discretion to those who need it. Then say . . .

> God make me a messenger for those I love.
> Let me carry their prayers as if they were my own,

*and leave them there, softly,*
*like bird's eggs, nesting in the crack of a wall,*
*awaiting the time for all they contain*
*to break out into joyous birth.*
*God grant me too*
*The merit to carry the means to Israel's redemption.*
*Until such time as we see the end of days,*
*God, make me a witness to history.*
*May I revel in its glories,*
*And relieve its pains.*
*In some small way, let this, my journey,*
*Awaken hope in those I love and those I barely know,*
*The people among whom I walk in the days ahead.*

בָּרוּךְ אַתָּה יְיָ אֱלֹהֵינוּ מֶלֶךְ הָעוֹלָם עֹשֶׂה צְדָקוֹת.

*Barukh atah Adonai Eloheinu melekh ha'olam,*
*oseh ts'dakot.*

Blessed is God, for acts of kindness.

## A Prayer for the Synagogue

People leaving on pilgrimage to Israel during the week to come are customarily given an *aliyah* in their synagogue, after which the following is recited by the rabbi or cantor on behalf of the congregation.

מִי שֶׁבֵּרַךְ אֲבוֹתֵינוּ,
אַבְרָהָם יִצְחָק וְיַעֲקֹב,
שָׂרָה, רִבְקָה, רָחֵל וְלֵאָה,
הוּא יְבָרֵךְ אֶת _____
הָעוֹמֵד/הָעוֹמֶדֶת לַעֲלוֹת
[יַחַד עִם מִשְׁפַּחְתּוֹ/מִשְׁפַּחְתָּהּ]
לְאֶרֶץ יִשְׂרָאֵל.
יְהִי רָצוֹן מִלְּפָנֶיךָ
שֶׁיִּסַּע/שֶׁתִּסַּע לְשָׁלוֹם,
וְשֶׁיַּגִּיעַ/וְשֶׁתַּגִּיעַ בְּשָׁלוֹם לְאֶרֶץ חֶמְדַּת לִבֵּנוּ,
לְאֶרֶץ צִיּוֹן.

יְהִי רָצוֹן מִלְּפָנֶיךָ שֶׁיַּחֲזֹר/שֶׁתִּתְחַזֹר אֵלֵינוּ
מְבֹרָךְ/מְבֹרֶכֶת בְּכָל מַעֲשָׂיו/מַעֲשֶׂיהָ,
מְחֻדָּשׁ/מְחֻדֶּשֶׁת מֵעַמֵּנוּ בִּמְדִינָתֵנוּ.

May the One who blessed our ancestors
 Abraham, Isaac and Jacob,
 Sarah, Rebekah, Rachel and Leah,
Bless_____
Who is about to ascend (with his/her family)
to the land of Israel.
May he/she travel there safely,
And arrive in peace to the land we hold dear,
 the land we call Zion.
May he/she return to us
 blessed in every undertaking
 inspired and renewed by our People in our land.
Tseitchem l'shalom, uvo'akhem l'shalom
We pray that you and all who go to Israel as you do,
May fly on angels' wings,
Transporting prayers of all this holy congregation
For life and peace.
To which we say . . . Amen!

# How to Shape Sacred Time

*or*

## *How to Prepare While on the Way*

For reading on the plane over to Israel.

You saw what I did . . .
how I carried you
on the wings of eagles.

—*Exodus 19:4*

Before your plane to Israel departs, recite *T'fillat Haderekh*, "Prayer for a Safe Journey" (p. 221). Then, during the flight, read the following.

## A. Finding (and Using) What You Want

### 1. This Place Is Holy (Section Four)

The centerpiece of this book is Section Four, "This Place Is Holy." It is a register of places, arranged according to four geographic regions, north, south, east, and west, following God's promise to Abraham.

> God said to Abram, "Raise your eyes and look out from where you are, *tsafonah v'negbah v'kedmah v'yamah,* to the North and South, to the East and West, for I give all the land that you see to you and your ancestors forever" (Genesis 13:14–15).

The places are listed in the Table of Contents, as well as alphabetically in the Index.

The list includes the spiritual sites that you are most likely to visit. For each one, it provides opportunities to *anticipate, approach,* and *acknowledge* the site (see pp. 49–51). The pages for each place also have lots of empty space for you to record *afterthoughts*, your own spiritual diary of the memories in the making to which you will want to return from time to time, and that you will be able to share with those you love. (See pp. 53–54.)

Here are some tips on how to make the best use of the register of places.

- *Before traveling to any of the four geographic regions,* look through the Table of Contents for the places in that region to get a feel for the area as a whole.

- *Each night*, go over your itinerary for the next day and see if the places that you expect to visit are in the Index.

- *Anticipation:* Once you have located the page(s) where tomorrow's destination is found, spend some time the night before you go there reading the Anticipation section. It generally gives you a feel for the place so that you will appreciate it better when you get there.

- *Approach:* Think of places as having a *focus* and a *vicinity*. For your guests whom you invite over for dinner, for example, your house is the focus of their trip; your neighborhood is the vicinity. The Wall in Jerusalem is a focus; a large surrounding empty square from which the Wall can be seen but not yet experienced, is the vicinity. We naturally feel our adrenaline rise when we know we are in the *vicinity* and the *focus* is near.

  When you arrive at the vicinity, or in the car or bus on your way to the site, read the paragraph marked *Approach.* This is usually an evocative poem or reading, often from the Bible, the Talmud, or the writings of a pilgrim who came here before you. It will give you a spiritual sense of the place's ambiance.

- *Acknowledgment:* It is traditional to say blessings immediately prior to the experience for which the blessing exists, as a way of greeting the experience in question and integrating it into consciousness. The experience usually occurs when you come face to face with the *focus,* not just the general *vicinity* in which the focus is found. Each site's Acknowledgment section is preceded by a suggestion as to where the Acknowledgment prayer should be said. But you need not limit yourself to the suggestion. If you prefer, whenever you feel yourself to be at the *focus*—the spiritual center of the site—stop where you are, and acknowledge its presence with the section marked Acknowledgment.

- *Guide to Blessing:* There is no way to know for sure all the places you will visit, or the thoughts and emotions that any one of them will evoke within you. Also, some blessings and readings are intended for more than one place. Before the plane lands, therefore, look through the Guide to Blessing (Section Five). It contains special readings intended for more than a single place: for "a place of beauty," for instance, or "a place of prayer," and so on. You may want to use these blessings over and over again, as you go from place to place.

- *Time alone:* At every place, take some time to be alone with the site, your book, yourself and God. Formulate some reflections, reactions or observations to record later as your Afterthoughts.

- *Afterthoughts:* Do not delay writing your thoughts down. You will be amazed how quickly you forget what you wanted to say when the experience was fresh in your mind.

## 2. The Guide to Blessing (Section Five)

Places are fixed in space. We have the luxury of traveling back and forth among them, visiting, revisiting, scheduling and anticipating. Time, on the other hand, comes but once, and is gone forever after. We try to plan it, but we never know exactly what the next moment may bring.

You will know well in advance, therefore, what places you can expect to visit, but you will never know for sure what opportunities you will have to greet a special moment that will come with fleeting immediacy and then vanish.

On one of my trips to Israel, for instance, I found myself in a Roman Catholic retreat house where I had been invited to lecture just before and after the holiday of Shavuot. Knowing that Shavuot is a pilgrim festival on which the Torah prescribes traveling to Jerusalem to eat and celebrate, I asked an Israeli acquaintance with a car to do me the favor of stopping at a bakery along the way to buy some pastry. Lunch hour in the retreat house was normally spent eating together, and time was allotted for announcements by tour guides, leaders of study expeditions, and the like. With some 100 guests from around the world gathered around me, none of whom I knew personally, I rose and invited everyone to share in my great joy at being able to fulfill this biblical commandment to be in Jerusalem at the time of the pilgrimage festival and to eat of the sweetness of the land. One by one, people came forward as their own lunch ended to request a piece of my pastry. As they ate, some thanked me, some thanked God, some offered me blessings, some just smiled, but all looked deeply into my eyes knowing that a precious moment had passed among us.

The Guide to Blessing is your reference to those special moments that tend to come some time during everyone's pilgrimage. I mean such things as catching a desert flower in full bloom, or standing in a place where miraculous events transpired once upon a time. These are awe-inspiring episodes of the ordinary, the burning bushes of our time, and Jewish tradition provides blessings for them.

You will want to know in advance what these blessings are or, at least, that a blessing exists, since the event in question may occur so unexpectedly that you will not have much time to find out what Jewish tradition provides for you to say. The Guide to Blessing therefore provides blessings for "generic" occasions. *Before your plane lands, spend some time with this section so that you have some idea of the blessings.* When you find yourself at a spot where you are moved to say a blessing, you may recall that it exists, and be able to look it up in time to use it.

The pages in Section Five contain suggestions as to where some of these time-bound blessings might be said. But these are only suggestions. Who knows when the right opportunity will arise? Be prepared! Do not let sacred moments pass. They never come again.

### 3. A Meal in Jerusalem (Section Six)

A special section is allotted to the single experience that has most typified a Jewish pilgrimage to Israel: sharing a meal of thanksgiving and celebration on sacred soil. It is suggested for Jerusalem, since Torah itself commands us to go there and eat with friends or family in the confines of the city that has consistently represented the final goal of every pilgrim's dream. In Second Temple times, a regular stream of visitors came from all around to do just that.

Section Six therefore provides a set of mealtime prayers, including a *Birkat Hamazon,* Grace after Meals. The version of blessings included is not entirely the same as the one you may be used to using back home, because it comes directly out of the body of ancient prayers found in the Cairo *Genizah*. They are part of the liturgy used by Jews in *Eretz Yisrael* before they fled from the Crusaders in 1099. By the time they returned, often several generations later, they had exchanged their ancient way of prayer for the customs they had discovered in the Diaspora. Only at the beginning of the twentieth century did archeologists discover manuscripts of their original prayers buried in the sands of time.

Who would have believed, when our ancestors fled from the approaching Crusaders, that their descendants would return some day to our land and make their prayers our own? The physical bodies of those Jews may have perished, but their spirit has not. When you say these prayers, you will be saying words that have not been said for 1,000 years.

It has always been a mitzvah of the highest order for pilgrims to eat in Jerusalem, thereby celebrating their homecoming and thanking God for the bounty available to them. Plan, therefore, at least one meal together as a group, and recapture as your own the prayers that Jews recited when they lived in Israel long ago.

### 4. Afterward: Keeping a Journal as Memories in the Making

Sections Four (This Place Is Holy) and Five (Guide to Blessing) provide space in which to record your response to where you have been and what you have done. Journal writing is a lost art. Most of us use the phone for personal calls, and limit letter writing to business matters. Our most profound and personal thoughts often pass fleetingly through our minds, and then get strangled before emerging full-blown in all their glory. But the Rabbis say that the very air of *Eretz Yisrael* makes us wise. This, after all, is the land of the prophets and judges of Israel, the men and women who were seized by inspiration that they never expected. You may be surprised to discover how deep your own thoughts are.

Take fifteen minutes each night to write them down, *even if they do not seem deep at the time.* You may feel that you have nothing to say, but you do. To begin with, your notes will help you remember what to tell the folks back home.

But in addition, think how grateful you would be if you could have a diary that your grandparents had composed. Now is your chance to keep a diary for people who come after you.

Record how you felt. Or, if you like, compose a poem, draw a picture, or write your own prayer. Do something with your thoughts, and you will have a memento more precious than any souvenir you might buy: a journal of your own interior landscape that you might never have known you had, something to read and reread back home, a diary to pass on to posterity.

## B. The Jewish Dimension

### 1. Blessings

As you discovered in your preparatory reading (pp. 51–53), the most important part of this book are the blessings for the times you come face to face with the sites and history of Israel. To appreciate what you are saying, you need to know a little more about where the blessings come from.

Like *T'fillat Haderekh*, the prayer for a safe journey, many of the blessings come directly from our standard prayer book, the *Siddur*. Others never made it to the *Siddur*, but can be found buried in ancient texts like the Talmud, codified for all time by the sages who set Judaism on its course centuries ago. Others never even made it to the Talmud. Our "official" Jewish books, the Talmud included, are only part of the Jewish heritage. We have, in addition, unofficial records, like diaries of pilgrims such as you, or writings by pious men and women of many eras whose words remained marginal to the official collection of rabbinic literature, but have been rediscovered by scholars in our time.

Of special relevance is the magnificent cache of ancient documents that I mentioned briefly above: the Cairo *Genizah*, with its spiritual heritage of *Eretz Yisrael* from Crusader times. When the Crusader armies from France, England and Germany arrived in Israel in 1099, they conquered the land, and established what they called the Latin Kingdom of Jerusalem. Most Jews fled or were expelled, but they returned about a century later, when the kingdom finally fell. In the interim, their native spiritual legacy, born of Jewish life in Israel for almost 1,000 years, was lost in the dust of time.

At the turn of this century, archaeologists exploring an old synagogue in Cairo, Egypt, stumbled upon a whole library of documents, miraculously saved by the arid climate there. To their surprise, the cache was a paper trail of Jewish life before and after the Crusaders arrived, and among its tatters of pages piled knee deep all over the floor were prayers from the community that the Crusaders expelled. They had apparently been taken to Egypt, where they had been relegated to museum-like status and forgotten. This book reproduces some of those fragments, as well as whatever else we know about the spiritual life of Jews in Israel 1,000 years ago.

In our time, we have recovered the physical heritage of the land. We have rebuilt it, making it again our own. So too, with this book, we recover the blessings and prayers that our forebears in Israel used to say over 1,000 years ago. We say again these, their prayers, in Israel, their land, affirming that both land and prayers are ours as well.

### 2. Endnotes for Depth
Yes, there are endnotes, but not the scholarly kind. Usually they tell you where the blessings are from. Make sure to use them to appreciate what you are saying.[1]

## C. The Personal Dimension

### 1. Know Your Trip
Whether you are traveling by yourself or in a group, you will have to find time to be alone with the places you visit rather than in the midst of busy crowds listening to historical lectures on what you are seeing. You should do the following:

- You can easily manage the Anticipation and Approach parts of your pilgrimage. Do these as indicated, reading the Anticipation the night before and the Approach while traveling to the place in question.

- The problem comes with the Acknowledgment. If you

are traveling as part of a group, it may not occur to anyone else to stop and say a blessing, and you will not be given time to thumb through this book to find what you want while everyone else continues on their way touring. You will therefore have to know in advance what blessing to say. Use a bookmark to have your book ready for the moment you arrive.

- As soon as you arrive at the place's focus, and feel the sense of its presence, open your book and stop to say your blessing.

- *Take your time; do it right; treat your spiritual impulses seriously.* Above all, *don't be shy*. You have the right to go off by yourself (within the bounds of safety), to linger behind briefly, or to ask the rest of your group to wait a moment until the impact of the event has been fully realized. The apt expression here is *derekh eretz*, the Jewish value of "respect for others." Spirituality is often intensely personal, so you should not expect that everyone will want to do exactly what you do or to take as much time doing it. Within the bounds of *derekh eretz*, however, the others will appreciate your taking these spiritual moments seriously, even if this means asking them to wait silently for the minute it takes to finish the page you are on, close your eyes to meditate, or open your eyes to let a tear flow undisturbed. (They would not think twice about asking you to wait a minute while they take another picture, or ask another question of the guide.) Spirituality is contagious; empower yourself to appreciate the sacred, and you will empower those with you to do the same.

You will then be ready to listen to your guide or to continue on the way along with the others. Most tours give you some private time after the official *"schpiel"* is over. Other people will use it to ask questions or just to wander around. This is a wonderful chance to be alone and think through what you may want to record as an Afterthought in your diary after you leave.

If you are on a tour or with a group in which everyone is using this book, you have the chance to organize each day to get the most out of the places you visit. You can pause

together as a group, as everyone approaches and acknowl-
edges the sites.

Remember that some places (especially Jerusalem)
have more than one site where a blessing is in order. Sacred
sites tend to cluster together in space the way holy days do in
time. Like the High Holy Days of Rosh Hashanah and Yom
Kippur, Israel is a High Holy Place, within which particular
locations loom especially rich in the presence of the holy.
Any given place may call for more than one blessing. One
site may appear in This Place is Holy (Section Four); another may not, but it may nonetheless evoke a blessing from
the Guide to Blessing (Section Five). Do not feel that you
have to hurry. Spend the time it takes to see and to say whatever the spiritual moments prompt.

### 2. Overcome Your Jewish Education

You may be struck in Israel at how little you know about
Judaism. Worse yet, you may discover that the Jewish school-
ing of your youth actually discouraged the experience of the
spiritual, to the point where you are hesitant about giving
yourself over to the sacredness of Israel. Treating it as history is easy. But as the place of God? Well. . . .

Up above, I discussed the dilemma you may have if you
are on a tour with strangers, and you are the only person with
this book. But oddly enough, people are usually least shy with
strangers. It may be the people we know and love most
whom we are afraid to startle with our new-found spiritual
impulses. Parents who are not accustomed to saying prayers
except in congregational settings are often afraid to pray in
front of their children, to the point where they cannot get
themselves to do so—in which case, the children lose almost
as much as their parents do. No matter what formal Jewish
education you have given your children, you will find that
it is less powerful in guaranteeing their Jewish future than
the example you set yourself; children are moved by the
experience of parents who are willing to stumble through an
unfamiliar prayer or two, rather than feign cool detachment
in the face of what matters most. Some of us are afraid even
to put our arm around the people we love, lest we cry publicly, or they get a glimpse of the softness we have hidden
for so long inside our normal efficient exterior. Others still

will concede that children need spiritual models, but will merely condescend to the kids, never open themselves up to the experience of the sacred for their own sake as adults— not publicly, anyway.

*Avoid the mistake of retaining your cool.* Whenever you use this book, make a point of doing so without embarrassment. If you want to, go off a few steps to be alone. Alone does not mean lonely, and you may find the experience of being alone with your thoughts and prayers of inestimable value. If the thought strikes you, ask someone you know to say "Amen!" after your blessing. You would ask them to take your picture, wouldn't you? Saying "Amen" takes a lot less time and is much easier. If you are with someone you love, you might even ask them to say the blessing with you, or just to hold your hand while you do so.

### 3. Be Creative

It never fails to amaze me how rational and competent adults, who organize families, care for children, attend to crises, and run businesses, somehow manage to revert to infancy when faced with religion. Our synagogues have often reduced us to passive observers or lemming-like fol-lowers of whatever the experts say and do. That wasn't the way the Rabbis of old meant things to turn out.

Once upon a time, there was no printing press, not even paper on which to scribble notes. Unable to have a handy pocket-size prayer book around, people were encour-aged to master the *art* of saying their own blessings, more than the rote practice of repeating the precise wording of blessings that other people had already made up. To be sure, we now have both paper and printing technology, so we can have in hand the age-old blessings made doubly precious by the very fact that thirty generations and more have said them. But we have every right to make up new ones ourselves.

This is, admittedly, a liberal approach to Jewish tradition. Rabbis living after the year 1000 tended to use the blessings that were already available from earlier rabbinic literature, so that the codes of Jewish law prohibit inventing new bless-ings for occasions that the Talmud never envisioned. People who follow Jewish law in its full and literal detail will hesitate to compose blessings they think Jewish law prohibits.

We know, however, that even after the year 1000, many Jews did, in practice, write their own blessings. And even those who did not write actual blessings complete with the formal introductory formula, "*Barukh atah Adonai Eloheinu melekh ha'olam*," did not hesitate to write prayers in freely composed prose or poetry.

Still, in practice, we rarely see new blessings still being composed today, and it cannot be denied that Jewish law (*halakhah*) prohibits the use of made-up blessings, for fear that by using blessings loosely, we may be taking God's name in vain. On the other hand, we are encouraged to recognize God in all we do. Liberally minded Jews may prefer to follow the precedent of people in the Middle Ages who wrote new blessings despite the technical prohibition against them, on the grounds that saying blessings is central to Jewish spirituality. They may argue that even the Talmud would allow them to do so in this day and age. Most Orthodox (and some Conservative) authorities, however, will permit new blessings only if the phrase that introduces them is shortened to omit God's name and the reference to God's rulership. Instead of saying the whole phrase, "*Barukh atah Adonai Eloheinu melekh ha'olam*" ("Blessed are You, Adonai our God, ruler of the world . . .") they advocate saying only "*Barukh atah*" ("Blessed are You"), or using the English translation alone.

In sum:

- Decide what your own parameters are. But whatever you do, do not feel that you must limit yourself to what you find in the pages here.

- If you want to make up blessings, note how easy it is; just say:

בָּרוּךְ אַתָּה יְיָ אֱלֹהֵינוּ מֶלֶךְ הָעוֹלָם

*or*

בָּרוּךְ אַתָּה

*Barukh atah Adonai Eloheinu melekh ha'olam*
or
*Barukh atah*

Blessed is God who . . . (add whatever seems right to you).

### 4. The Sacred and the Everyday

It has often been said that Judaism is a religion of the everyday. It is not that we are intent on transforming the everyday into the sacred. It is that the sacred exists around every ordinary bend in life's journey. Our daily prayer acknowledging the miracles of God, for instance, does not specify the spectacular instances of the hand of God. Instead, you find mention of "Your miracles which are with us daily, the wonders and goodness that occur all the time—morning, noon and night." On the great occasions that recollect God's miracles—Passover, for instance—we say a set of psalms called the *Hallel*, prayers of gratitude and awe at what God has done. But every day begins with such a set of prayers; the ordinary morning service starts with a lengthy section called *Hallel Sheb'khol Yom*—the Daily *Hallel*.

Jews are trained to look for God in ordinary places: faces on the street, blossoms on a tree, a simple loaf of bread. Remember Elijah as he heads to the wilderness to find God:

> Then, lo, the Lord passed by. There was a great and mighty wind, splitting mountains and shattering rocks by the power of the Lord. But the Lord was not in the wind. After the wind, an earthquake; but the Lord was not in the earthquake. After the earthquake, fire; but the Lord was not in the fire. And after the fire—a still, small voice (1 Kings 18:11–12).

Blessings are our own still small voice, the best approximation we have to being Godlike ourselves. They are an act of creation, that convert the ordinary into the extraordinary, not because they are a kind of verbal alchemy turning leaden experience into gold, but because they reveal the sacred in the everyday.

Here is your first blessing. Try saying it now:

בָּרוּךְ אַתָּה יְיָ אֱלֹהֵינוּ מֶלֶךְ הָעוֹלָם
הַמֵּכִין מִצְעֲדֵי גָבֶר.

*Barukh atah Adonai Eloheinu melekh ha'olam,*
*hameichin mitsadei gaver.*

Blessed is God who sets us firmly upon our way.[2]

## 5. Prayers for Arrival

### Anticipation

(To be recited shortly before landing.)

*I've seen the old-time films of how they kiss the ground,*
*Those old-time Jews unblemished by sophistication.*
*As for me, well, I'll just look around, unexcited-like,*
*Cool as a cucumber.*
*(Or maybe as a m'lah-f'foan, as they call cucumbers*
*    here.)*
*This is just an airport where they lose your bags the same*
*    as any place on earth,*
*But in Hebrew.*
*I've heard the tales of Jews who burst out crying on these*
*    shores,*
*Middle-aged men from the Middle Ages, mostly,*
*Who had a thing for tears, I guess—*
*It was a wailing wall, back then, where they cried each*
*    day at sunrise and at sunset,*
*And watched and waited for the Ninth of Av, with special*
*    joy, for all I know,*
*Because they could cry more then.*
*But as for me, well, thank you, I don't cry a lot,*
*Not even in Jerusalem,*
*Let alone in Tel Aviv, where (after all)*
*People plod to work, smoke cigarettes, drink Coca Cola*
*(Koa-kah koa-lah, as they call it here—*
*Who says I can't speak Hebrew?)*
*But then again, I've never really come like this,*
*Never stood here, all alone with just my jet-lagged*
*    thoughts*
*On what I should be careful not to do,*
*In case someone is watching.*
*Who doesn't wonder what it was like*
*To embrace the ground*
*And steal at least a single kiss,*
*From the dust of Israel's past,*
*The way they did*
*When pre-jet props used runways made of smoothed-out*
*    sacred soil, instead of tarmac?*

בָּרוּךְ אַתָּה יְיָ אֱלֹהֵינוּ מֶלֶךְ הָעוֹלָם מְכוֹפֵף זְקוּפִים.

*Barukh atah Adonai Eloheinu melekh ha'olam,*
*m'khofef z'kufim.*

Blessed is God, who lets us fall upon our knees.[3]

## Acknowledgment

*1. On arriving safely*
(To be said as the plane comes to a stop.)

בָּרוּךְ אַתָּה יְיָ אֱלֹהֵינוּ מֶלֶךְ הָעוֹלָם
הַגּוֹמֵל לְחַיָּבִים טוֹבוֹת שֶׁגְּמָלַנִי כָּל טוֹב.

*Barukh atah Adonai Eloheinu melekh ha'olam,*
*hagomel l'chayavim tovot sheg'malani kol tov.*

Blessed is God, who does favors even for the
undeserving, and has treated me so kindly.[4]

*2. For the road from the airport to Jerusalem . . .*
(The airport is near the Mediterranean coast. But very
shortly, the car taking you to Jerusalem will turn
inland, and then, just short of the city, you begin to
climb a long road upward—up to the sacred center of
the Jewish universe! If you can, ask your driver to stop
along the way, perhaps near the rusted remains of the
armored vehicles that were left as visible reminders of
the fight for independence in 1948. Then read the following:)

### On the Road to Jerusalem

The drivers of these vehicles were not pilgrims, not
like us. Nor were they tourists. They were warriors
with guns, not cameras. It was 1948, and Jerusalem
was surrounded by enemy troops intent on stran-
gling the city into submission. Its survival depended on a daily convoy carrying food up what was
then a narrow mountain road guarded on both sides
by enemy fire. Slowly but inexorably, the amount
of food that got through tailed off to a fraction of

what was needed, so in March, the Haganah mounted a large convoy of forty trucks. Guarded in the front and rear by armored vehicles, this was a last-ditch attempt to break through the siege with flour, canned goods, and even oranges, for the 100,000 Jerusalemites who were completely cut off from all communication with the outside world.

Arab intelligence learned of the plan in time to mount an ambush. Stones that looked like an ordinary road block were outfitted with land mines that would explode when the convoy's leading vehicles pushed through. The trucks carrying food would then be trapped behind the metal debris and human remains from the lead vehicles, easy targets for the hand grenades that hidden soldiers carried on both sides of the road.

The attack went as planned. Hand grenades destroyed the trucks, forcing their drivers out onto the road. There they were met with bullets fired by Arab villagers from all along the road who had joined the regular troops in anticipated victory. What was left of the convoy managed to turn around or back down the hill to safety. But nineteen vehicles, roughly half of those which began the journey, were destroyed, their drivers and occupants killed. To this day, their rusted hulks have been left in sight, that all who enter Jerusalem may not take their journey here for granted.

### From *Psalm 25—Tanks and Planes Are Not the True Salvation* by Danny Siegel

*O Lord*
*We are chosen,*
*but weary of the tear soaked pages*
*of our history.*

*We ask nothing of You, Lord,*
*but opportunities to raise*
*carnations in the Negev*
*and a crop of cinnamon*
*in Galilee.*

(Facing Jerusalem at the top of the mountain road, add:)

עוֹד יִשָּׁמַע   *Od yishama*

בְּעָרֵי יְהוּדָה   *b'arei y'hudah*

וּבְחוּצוֹת יְרוּשָׁלַיִם   *uv'chutsot y'rushalayim*

קוֹל שָׂשׂוֹן וְקוֹל שִׂמְחָה,   *kol sason v'kol simchah*

קוֹל חָתָן וְקוֹל כַּלָּה.   *kol chatan v'kol kallah*

In the cities of Judah
And the courtyards of Jerusalem,
Let only this be heard:
   the sound of joy and happiness,
   weddings on every corner.[5]

בָּרוּךְ אַתָּה יְיָ אֱלֹהֵי דָּוִד בּוֹנֶה יְרוּשָׁלָיִם.

*Barukh atah Adonai, Elohei david, boneh
y'rushalayim.*

Blessed is the God of David, who builds up
Jerusalem.[6]

3. *For arriving at your destination in Jerusalem:*

בָּרוּךְ אַתָּה יְיָ אֱלֹהֵינוּ מֶלֶךְ הָעוֹלָם
שֶׁהֶחֱיָנוּ וְקִיְּמָנוּ וְהִגִּיעָנוּ לַזְּמַן הַזֶּה.

*Barukh atah Adonai Eloheinu melekh ha'olam,
shehecheyanu v'kiy'manu v'higiyanu lazman
hazeh.*

Blessed is God for granting us life, for sustaining
us, and for bringing us to this moment.

4. *Before retiring for the first night in Israel*
(The following may be said alone, but is intended,
preferably, for the whole group to say together before
dispersing for the night.)

*Oh God,*
*How far we've traveled, just for this,*
*To be just here,*
*Precisely here, at this most sacred place,*
*Exactly now, at this most sacred time*

*for which we have devoutly hoped—and worked—and*
     *waited.*
*And so we pray for every happy circumstance that you*
     *may bless us with.*
*Help us cling dearly to this moment of our lives,*
*To hold it softly in our hands, and then, to fit it firmly in*
     *its place in memory.*
*Help us in the days ahead*
*To wend our way through history.*
*Help us hear the echo of the words heard by prophets,*
*Of dry bones rising or of David's wild dance on his way*
     *to Jerusalem.*
*As we go from place to place*
*May we go from strength to strength,*
*And find the words to offer silent prayers to You*
*Of time gone by, or yet to come,*
*Assured by the knowledge*
*That moments truly marked by prayer can never vanish in*
     *the wind.*

בָּרוּךְ אַתָּה יְיָ הַמְחַדֵּשׁ יָמֵינוּ כְּקֶדֶם.

*Barukh atah Adonai, ham'chadesh yameinu*
*k'kedem.*

Blessed is God, who renews our days as of old.[7]

# This Place Is Holy

*or*

## *What to Say at Specific Places*

God said to Abram, "Raise your eyes
and look out from where you are,
*tsafonah v'negbah v'kedmah v'yamah*,
to the north and south, to the east and
west, for I give all the land that you see
to you and your ancestors forever."

—*Genesis 13:14–15*

## This Place Is Holy

God said to Abram, "Raise your eyes
and look out from where you are,
*tsafonah v'negbah v'kedmah v'yamah,*
to the north and south, to the east and west,
for I give all the land that you see
to you and your ancestors forever."
—*Genesis 13:14–15*

# THE GALIL:
## *"Tsafonah—to the North"*

# Deganya, Kibbutz in the Galil, Or Cemetery of Chalutzim (Pioneers) at the Kinneret (Sea of Galilee)

You shall eat of the labor of your hands.

—*Psalm 128:2*

## Anticipation

Visit the *kibbutzim* up north around the *Kinneret,* especially Deganya (if you can) or go to the cemetery where the air is thick with memories of the *chalutzim*, the pioneers, whose legendary exploits and not-so-legendary labor created Israel out of nothing. Once this was mostly malaria-infested swampland. Now it is lush farmland. Kibbutz Deganya is the grandfather of the Kibbutz Movement, alive still with memories of A. D. Gordon (1856–1922) who gave modern Israel its ideology of sacred labor, and of Rachel Blaustein (1890–1931), "a young delicate girl from Russia," as Golda Meir remembered her, both a poet and a worker.

Gordon actually made aliyah alone, bringing his wife and daughter only five years later. Though he had never done an ounce of manual labor in his life, he plunged into backbreaking fieldwork in the vineyards and orange groves, contracted malaria, nearly died of starvation, but through it all, developed a theory of "the religion of labor."

Rachel (as she signed her poetry) came from Russia, fell under the spell of Gordon's revolutionary mysticism of labor, and returned briefly to France to study agriculture. Her education completed, she was forced to wait out World War I in Russia, where she taught children to make aliyah as she herself intended to do as soon as the war ended. Once in Israel, however, Rachel found that she had contracted tuberculosis, and simply could not work the land she loved so well. The world is grateful for her poetry now, but as Golda Meir, concludes, "This was her sorrow: that she could not do physical work."

The poetry of Israel echoes with the ideal of work that was so central to the psyche of the early immigrants, especially those from the Second and Third Aliyah, and who established the labor movement and the *kibbutzim*.[1] The religious love-affair they had with physical labor comes through clearly in the poem you will read tomorrow, by Abraham Shlonsky. Shlonsky a Ukrainian Jew, made aliyah in 1921. When not writing poetry, he worked on a construction gang and described himself as the "road-paving poet of Israel."

## Approach

### From the Writings of A.D. Gordon

I awake with a start and shake off that life that was over me and within me. I commence all things anew. I begin at the beginning. The first thing that opens my heart to a life such as I have not yet known is work. Not work for a livelihood, not work in obedience to a command, but work upon which a new light shines. This work, which I see is a part of life, one of life's deepest roots. So I work. . . .

As I keep working, suffering, there is no drop of my blood, no ounce of my strength or intellect, which perishes uselessly. For every drop of blood is a spark of fire, and every ounce of strength or intellect is a spark of light to my soul which is being regenerated. . . . Our claim to the Land rests on whatever the Land or its life gains through our labor. . . . We seek life, nothing more or less, our own life, from our own life-source, from the nature of the Land. . . . We come to the Land to be imbedded in its natural soil from which we were uprooted, through our roots to draw sustenance from the earth, through our leaves to breathe in nourishment from the winds and from the creative power that lies in the rays of light.

At times you imagine that you too are taking root in the soil that you are digging; like all that is growing around, you are nurtured by the light of the sun's rays with food from heaven. You feel that you too live a life in common with the tiniest blade of grass, with each flower, each tree; that you live deeply in the heart of nature, rising up from it all and growing straight up into the expanse of the world . . . .

If we do not till the soil with our own hands, the soil will not be ours—the Land will not be ours, and we will not be the People of the Land. Even here we shall be aliens, just as in the lands of the Diaspora where, too, there are Jews who rent land, who buy fields, gardens, and orchards, but who traffic in the fruit and labor of others. . . . We cannot deceive ourselves much longer in the belief that investing money in business, parceling out work, and superintending affairs constitutes the essence of labor, the essence of such national creativity as will give us title to the Land.

One must first of all abandon the ordinary point of view: that which seemed to be the essentials of life, the pleasantness of life, the why and wherefore of life. It is useless to search for a new life, unless one's attitude toward life is transformed. A new life predicates a new zest for life. Palestine is more than a worn-out holiday costume, more than a means for an economic existence, more than a kind of business enterprise. We should judge it by the standard reserved for our ancient dream: redemption.[2]

## Acknowledgment

(To be said, perhaps, in the fields of a kibbutz.)

### Toil, Abraham Shlonsky

*Dress me, good mother, in a robe of many colors.*
*Lead me at dawn to work.*

*My land is wrapped in light, as in a tallit.*
*The houses stand out like t'fillin boxes.*
*The roads, paved by hand, stream out like t'fillin*
*    straps.*

*Here the lovely city davens Shacharit to its creator.*
*And among its creators is your son, Abraham,*
*A road-building poet in Israel.*

*At evening twilight, father returns from his labor,*
*And whispers pleasantly, as if in prayer,*
Haben yakir li Avraham[3]
*Abraham is a dear son to me;*
*skin, sinews, and bones.*
*Hallelujah!*

*Dress me, good mother, in a robe of many colors.*
*Lead me at dawn to work.*

בָּרוּךְ אַתָּה יְיָ אֱלֹהֵינוּ מֶלֶךְ הָעוֹלָם
הַמְּכוֹנֵן מַעֲשֵׂי יָדֵינוּ.

*Barukh atah Adonai Eloheinu melekh ha'olam,*
*ham'khonen ma'aseh yadeinu.*

**Blessed is God, who establishes the work of our hands.[4]**

(If you have an opportunity to eat at the kibbutz, see special prayers for the occasion, p. 215.)

*Afterthoughts*

# Jezreel Valley

I love you, I love every tree we planted,
every clod of this earth.

—*Pioneering founder of the valley,*
*Manya Shochat, on her death bed*

## Anticipation

The Jezreel is Israel's largest inland valley, connecting east to west just south of the northland called the Galil. The biblical judge, Gideon, selected his troops in the spring of Harod (now a national park area) and at nearby En Dor (now a kibbutz), King Saul consulted a soothsayer before fighting his last battle on Mount Gilboa, which dominates the valley's southern rim. Pompey passed through in 63 B.C.E., building up Bet Shean, still the site of a magnificent Roman ampitheatre, and Napoleon followed him some 1,800 years later. The valley returned to Jewish hands with the establishment of the pioneer settlement of Merchavia in 1911.

The valley is home to famous mothers in Israel. Here Deborah the prophet subdued the Canaanites with the help of Ya'el, whom the Bible calls, "most blessed of women" for her military valor. Modern times produced Manya Shochat, a member of the pioneering group known as *Hashomer*, "The Watchers." Manya's biographer draws a vivid picture of the early years.

"A feeling of wonderment filled Manya as she watched her friends who first furrowed the land of the valley. From that moment in time, the valley was theirs. Manya participated in its colonization; its glorious moments as well as its times of threat, ceaselessly concerning herself with her friends in their ramshackle huts. The *Hashomer* members settled that land with superhuman self-sacrifice. Their first dwellings were of clay, only windowless huts, crawling with mice. Near them was a communal oven. Later on shacks were constructed and the place was renamed Merchavia."

Among other things, Manya served as treasurer. A 1911 letter back home to the Lovers of Zion foundation in Russia gives you a sense of just how tenuous the whole enterprise was.

"In response to your telegram, we are sending you a short analysis of *Hashomer*—about its meteoric rise, its multiple needs, and about the urgent requirement to set up a foundation which will free us from our constant supplications to the government. We will speak more of this in the future but for now, we will address the issue of how vital these 2,000 francs are for us, which we entreat you to wire us immediately. From the money which *Hashomer* received this year, we have the following balance:

| | |
|---|---|
| Surety fund | Fr 4,000 |
| Arms | Fr 1,400 |
| Assistance Fund | Fr 1,300 |
| 11 horses | Fr 30,000 |

(One horse was shot in an Arab attack.)"

You can still visit any or all of these places. When you do, cast your eyes around the valley to remember the sacrifice that went into it—from Deborah to Manya, a period spanning 3,000 years of history.

## Approach

### The Harshness of the Pioneer Years,
### by Anna Shochat, Manya's daughter

One of the central things was work and hard labor. To stand on your own, to work, to earn a living, to help others and to be a working laboring group. As children we practically did not learn, just worked, beginning from the age of five, from six in the morning. I do not remember vacation at all, only work. We, the children, were responsible for the sheep. We would milk the goats at ten and four and in between took them to graze. We could never go far because we had to get back for milking. We also

did seasonal work, cleaning and threshing and shep-
herding—and always barefoot.

Another important tenet was loyalty. Not to
inform and not to tell our friends. There were
weapons, and we heard many stories that if they
catch you and beat you, you must stand firm in the
tortures and not tell. . . . We spent entire nights in
the storehouse cleaning the bullets and shining
them, removing the rust and making piles and piles.
. . . We learned to handle weapons at the age of
eleven, to dismantle and assemble rifles. Then there
were exercises with guns, like taking them apart in
the dark with our eyes closed. We practiced in the
hayloft, but there was another special place, a secret
place that we did not even dare to say its name out
loud. Secrecy and loyalty were holy values. And this
loyalty, this unwillingness ever to inform on a friend
extended itself into also being always ready to help
others.

We, the children of the kibbutz, grew up in two
houses, six–seven to a room. There weren't enough
beds, and we would sleep four in a bed. I still
remember sleeping four in a bed head to toe, and
we would remove the thorns from each other's feet
because we were always barefoot.

I saw my mother cry once. I was ill with typhus.
I was eleven years old. The fever kept going up. At
first they thought I had malaria. I had six attacks. I
remember lying there. They came in to take my
temperature. The thermometer was in my hand, not
even under my arm and the temperature was 42°C
[over 105°F]. I was delirious, and they put ice on my
body and the ice kept melting. I remember my
mother sitting there with tears running down her
face. I felt myself passing away, but somehow, I mus-
tered up some strength and survived.

Many have asked what I did after four o'clock
when all the children went to their parents. I had
nowhere to go. I felt that I had nothing, that I was
all alone. I pitied myself, but never really gave it serious thought. Mixed up with my feelings of not
being good enough was the concept of the homeland. And my parents carried the burden of the
homeland relentlessly on their backs. Once during
one of the festivals, Ben-Gurion asked me some-

thing about my parents, and I told him that I was an orphan. I don't know how those words escaped, but he got angry and said that I should not dare speak like that again, that thanks to my parents, the settlement exists.[5]

## Acknowledgment

(To be recited while standing in the valley, looking up at the surrounding mountains.)

*The Song of Deborah,* Judges 5:3,7

אָנֹכִי לַיהוה אָנֹכִי אָשִׁירָה,
אֲזַמֵּר לַיהוה אֱלֹהֵי יִשְׂרָאֵל.
חָדְלוּ פְרָזוֹן,
בְּיִשְׂרָאֵל חָדֵלּוּ,
עַד שַׁקַּמְתִּי דְּבוֹרָה,
שַׁקַּמְתִּי אֵם בְּיִשְׂרָאֵל.

*I will sing to the Lord*
*Will hymn the Lord the God of Israel. . . .*
*Deliverance ceased,*
*Ceased in Israel,*
*Until you arose, Deborah,*
*You arose a mother in Israel.*

בָּרוּךְ אַתָּה יְיָ עוֹשֶׂה אִמָהוֹת בְּיִשְׂרָאֵל.

*Barukh atah Adonai, oseh imahot b'yisrael*

Blessed is God, who establishes mothers in Israel.

*Afterthoughts*

# Safed

*Hin'ni mukhan um'zuman l'taken olam.*
Here I am ready and prepared to make the world whole again.

—Based on the thought of Isaac Luria,
the Holy Ari of blessed memory[6]

## Anticipation

Once commonly despised as superstitious nonsense, the Kabbalah has come into its own as a source of wisdom, deep beyond measure. If you spend one day in Safed, the home of Kabbalah, you will know why.

The narrow streets and alleyways seem to wind automatically to the synagogue of Rabbi Isaac Luria, known to posterity as the Ari, "the Lion," and also an acronym for Adoneino Rabbi Yitzchak, "Our master, Rabbi Isaac." He was the most influential genius of the many seers and sages who once walked these streets. They came mostly from Spain, remnants of the inquisition and expulsion, seeking answers to the chaos of their lives. They carried with them the *Zohar*, a thirteenth-century work of mystical meaning. The Ari and his circle proclaimed that a divine presence inhabits even the broken universe of tragedy and evil, awaiting the good work of human beings to mend the world. In the eighteenth century, this doctrine was adopted and expanded in Chasidism, and has recently reemerged as a modern mystical revival, the same search for meaning that haunted the Ari and his generation.

Across from the synagogue sits a cemetery considered by many to be the third most sacred site in all of Israel, just short of Jerusalem's *Kotel* and Temple mount, and perhaps Hebron. You will find your way down the stairs to the two large tombstones that dominate the old grave sites. One marks the resting place of the Ari himself; the other of Solomon Alkabetz, the author of the most famous synagogue Shabbat poem of all time: *L'kha Dodi,* "Come, my beloved to meet the [Shabbat] bride . . ."

## Approach

From *The Pious Customs of Isaac Luria* [7]

1. The most important of all worthy traits consists in an individual's behaving with humility, modesty and the fear of sin to the greatest possible degree. One should also to the utmost degree, remain at a distance from pride, anger, fussiness, foolishness and evil gossip. One should abstain from idle conversation and flying off the handle, even with members of one's own household.

2. Melancholia is, by itself, an exceedingly unpleasant personal quality, especially for people whose intention is to acquire esoteric knowledge and experience the Holy Spirit. Nothing impedes mystical inspiration—even for someone who is otherwise worthy of it—more than the quality of sadness.

3. Additionally, the quality of anger, aside from serving as an obstacle to mystical inspiration altogether [has other injurious repercussions]. My teacher, of blessed memory [the Ari] used to be more exacting when it came to anger than with all other transgressions, even in a situation where a person explodes in anger for the sake of some religious obligation. This is because all other transgressions injure only a single limb of the body, whereas the quality of anger injures the soul in its entirety, altering the character completely. This is the issue: when we lose our temper, the holy soul departs from us altogether. In its place there enters a soul of an evil nature. This is the esoteric meaning of the verse from Job (18:4) "You who tear yourself in your anger." Such a person actually tears the holy soul, rendering it unfit at the moment of wrath.

## Acknowledgment

(To be said while standing in the synagogue of the Ari or at his grave in the cemetery just below.)

*For the sake of the unification of the Holy One Blessed be He and his Sh'khinah, behold I perform the mitzvah of visiting Israel, in fear and love, love and fear, through the hidden and concealed One, in the name of all Israel, and in order to give satisfaction to my creator and maker, and in order to raise the Sh'khinah from the dust.*

בָּרוּךְ אַתָּה יְיָ אֱלֹהֵינוּ מֶלֶךְ הָעוֹלָם גּוֹאֵל יִשְׂרָאֵל.

*Barukh atah Adonai Eloheinu melekh ha'olam, go'el yisra'el.*

Blessed is God, redeemer of Israel.[8]

## Afterthoughts

# THE NEGEV:
## *"Negbah—to the South"*

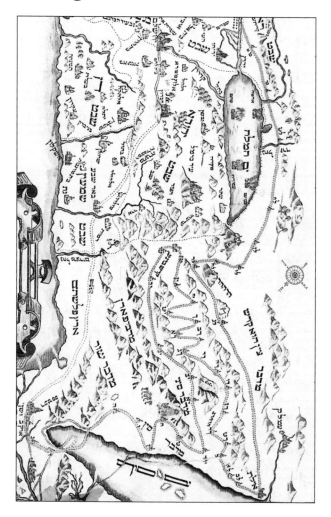

# Dead Sea and Sodom

The outrage of Sodom and Gomorrah is so great
and their sin so grave. . . .

—Genesis 18:20

## Anticipation

This is Israel's "Death Valley," a descent from the craggy
mountains to sea level and then beyond, reaching the lowest point in the earth's surface! Metaphorically too, it is the
low point of human existence, the location of Sodom and
Gomorrah, cities so sinful that they had to be destroyed from
the face of the earth. The Bible leaves little doubt about the
horrors that transpired here: rampant violence, sexual abuse
and licentiousness were common public practice. Abraham's
entreaty to save the town was insufficient because God could
not find even five good people there. In the end, angels
dressed like men were sent to destroy it.

> As dawn broke, the angels urged Lot [Abraham's
> nephew] saying, "Up, take your wife and your two
> remaining daughters, lest you be swept away by the
> iniquity of the city." Still, he delayed. So the men
> seized his hand and the hands of his wife and his
> two daughters—in the Lord's mercy on him—and
> brought him out and left him outside the city. When
> they brought him outside, one of them said, "Flee
> for your life. Do not look behind you, nor stop any-
> where along the Plain; flee to the hills. Lest you be
> swept away."
>
> The Lord rained upon Sodom and Gomorrah
> sulfurous fire from heaven. He annihilated those
> cities and the entire Plain. And all the inhabitants
> of the cities and the vegetation of the ground. Lot's
> wife, behind him, looked back, and she was there-
> upon turned into a pillar of salt (Genesis 19:15-17,
> 24–26).

The Dead Sea still bears her "name," in Hebrew—*Yam Hamelakh,* "The Salt Sea."

## *Approach*

*I've often wondered what Lot's wife saw,*
*Why she lost her soul for salt,*
*And now lies strewn around the water's edge, I*
*    guess,*
*part of its name, "The Salt Sea."*
*Was it wistfulness for her past,*
*Some secret urge to perpetuate the violence*
*At a distance,*
*At least to watch the city die*
*Like Mme. LaFarge who used to knit a stitch of*
*    pleasure*
*Each time the guillotine came slicing down.*

*The waters thick with salt and iodine and potash*
*And untold minerals fresh from some old chemistry*
*    textbook*
*Even smell like evil.*
*They boil up like tar in the hot desert sun.*
*Experience-starved tourists unload from buses to*
*    float in them,*
*Then shower endlessly to purge their skin*
*Of what the waters know deep down,*
*Of ancient human baseness.*

*I am no Mrs. Lot, but nonetheless, like her,*
*I cannot resist a backward glance at history here,*
*And I wonder . . .*
*Why have the Salt Sea's waters eroded so in recent*
*    years*
*(It's really just a puddle now compared to what it*
*    was)?*
*Could it be that when the Messiah comes*
*These waters thick with Sodom-memories will all*
*    dry up?*

## *Acknowledgment*

(To be said while looking out at the Dead Sea from its shores.)

עַל חֵטְא שֶׁחָטָאנוּ לְפָנֶיךָ
סְלַח לָנוּ מְחַל לָנוּ כַּפֶּר לָנוּ.

*Al chet shechatanu l'fanekha,*
*s'lakh lanu, m'chal lanu, kaper lanu.*

For the sins that we, the human race, have committed before You, God, forgive us, pardon us, grant us atonement.[9]

# Afterthoughts

# Ein Gedi

Streams come out of the rock,
waters flow down like rivers.

—*Psalm 78:16*

## Anticipation

Nothing heralds hope more than an oasis in the wilderness. Appropriately, then, not far from the Dead Sea where nothing grows, and with the memory of Sodom's bestiality still somehow lying heavily in the hot desert air, there is a sign of hope: the oasis of Ein Gedi. Already in the Stone Age, some 6,000 years ago, our ancestors were coming here for the abundant water and lush vegetation. King Saul came here hunting for David, whom he suspected of treason. When, to Saul's surprise, David spared Saul's life, after coming across him unarmed and vulnerable to attack, Saul proclaimed David's succession to the throne.

Ein Gedi is a place where it is easy to believe in a messianic coming. You climb away from desert waste and come to waterfalls that splash happily on picnickers who seem to have left all cares back in the desert sand. All around are shrubs and trees and cacti, practically inviting you to take their picture in the shininess of the midday sun.

If the sins of Sodom represent an image of inhumanity and its neighboring Dead Sea the epitome of death, Ein Gedi presents the positive pole of love and life. Its theme was recognized early in the Bible itself, when the anonymous author of the Song of Songs described Ein Gedi as the place best suited for making love.

Take the time to climb through Ein Gedi's paths up and out of the desert heat; let its cool clear water wash away all anxiety. Dream of the messianic promise of King David, and the sheer joy of love—life at its oasis best.

## Approach

*The Song of Songs, 1:2–8, 12–14*[10]

יִשָּׁקֵנִי מִנְּשִׁיקוֹת פִּיהוּ

כִּי טוֹבִים דֹּדֶיךָ מִיָּיִן:

לְרֵיחַ שְׁמָנֶיךָ טוֹבִים

שֶׁמֶן תּוּרַק שְׁמֶךָ

עַל כֵּן עֲלָמוֹת אֲהֵבוּךָ:

מָשְׁכֵנִי אַחֲרֶיךָ נָּרוּצָה

הֱבִיאַנִי הַמֶּלֶךְ חֲדָרָיו

נָגִילָה וְנִשְׂמְחָה בָּךְ

נַזְכִּירָה דֹּדֶיךָ מִיַּיִן

מֵישָׁרִים אֲהֵבוּךָ:

שְׁחוֹרָה אֲנִי וְנָאוָה

בְּנוֹת יְרוּשָׁלָיִם

כְּאָהֳלֵי קֵדָר

כִּירִיעוֹת שְׁלֹמֹה:

אַל תִּרְאֻנִי

שֶׁאֲנִי שְׁחַרְחֹרֶת

שֶׁשְּׁזָפַתְנִי הַשָּׁמֶשׁ:

הַגִּידָה לִּי שֶׁאָהֲבָה נַפְשִׁי

אֵיכָה תִרְעֶה

אֵיכָה תַּרְבִּיץ בַּצָּהֳרָיִם

שַׁלָּמָה אֶהְיֶה כְּעֹטְיָה

עַל עֶדְרֵי חֲבֵרֶיךָ:

אִם לֹא תֵדְעִי לָךְ הַיָּפָה בַּנָּשִׁים

צְאִי לָךְ בְּעִקְבֵי הַצֹּאן

וּרְעִי אֶת גְּדִיֹּתַיִךְ

עַל מִשְׁכְּנוֹת הָרֹעִים:

עַד שֶׁהַמֶּלֶךְ בִּמְסִבּוֹ

נִרְדִּי נָתַן רֵיחוֹ:

צְרוֹר הַמֹּר דּוֹדִי לִי

בֵּין שָׁדַי יָלִין:

אֶשְׁכֹּל הַכֹּפֶר דּוֹדִי לִי

בְּכַרְמֵי עֵין גֶּדִי:

*I long for his kiss; the kisses of his mouth!*
*Your love is better than wine.*
*Your anointing oil is fragrant,*
*Your name is perfume poured out.*
*No wonder the girls love you!*

*Take me along, quickly,*
*A king who admits me to his bedroom.*
*We will rejoice on your account,*
*Extol your love—better than wine.*
*For good reason they do love you!*

*I am black and beautiful,*
*O women of Jerusalem,*
*Like the tents of Kedar,*
*and the curtains of Solomon.*
*Will you stare at me with your eyes*
*Because I am dark*
*Because the sun has looked me through?*

*Tell me, O my deepest love,*
*Where you pasture your flock,*
*Where you lie them down at noon-time.*
*Why should I play hide-and-seek*
*Among the flocks of your friends?*

*If you do not know, most beautiful woman,*
*Follow the tracks of the flock*
*And pasture your kids*
*Where the shepherds lie. . . .*

*Before the king arrives at his couch,*
*My perfume hovered fragrantly.*
*My love will lie between my breasts.*
*Like a sack of myrrh,*
*A cluster of blossoms,*
*Picked from the vineyards of Ein Gedi.*

## Acknowledgment

(To be recited, if possible, at one of the waterfalls, preferably the highest one, where water cascades down into a pool of water.)

## Psalm 65: 9–13

וַיִּירְאוּ יֹשְׁבֵי קְצָוֹת מֵאוֹתֹתֶיךָ
מוֹצָאֵי בֹקֶר וָעֶרֶב תַּרְנִין:
פָּקַדְתָּ הָאָרֶץ וַתְּשֹׁקְקֶהָ
רַבַּת תַּעְשְׁרֶנָּה
פֶּלֶג אֱלֹהִים מָלֵא מָיִם
תָּכִין דְּגָנָם כִּי כֵן תְּכִינֶהָ:
תְּלָמֶיהָ רַוֵּה נַחֵת גְּדוּדֶיהָ
בִּרְבִיבִים תְּמֹגְגֶנָּה
צִמְחָהּ תְּבָרֵךְ:
עִטַּרְתָּ שְׁנַת טוֹבָתֶךָ
וּמַעְגָּלֶיךָ יִרְעֲפוּן דָּשֶׁן:
יִרְעֲפוּ נְאוֹת מִדְבָּר
וְגִיל גְּבָעוֹת תַּחְגֹּרְנָה:

*You visit the earth and water it,*
*You greatly enrich it.*
*The river of God is full of water;*
*You provide the people with grain,*
*For so You have prepared it.*
*You water its furrows abundantly,*
*Settling its ridges,*
*Softening it with showers,*
*And blessing its growth.*
*You crown the year with your bounty,*
*Your wagon tracks overflow with richness.*
*The pastures of the wilderness overflow.*
*The hills gird themselves with joy.*
*The meadows clothe themselves with flocks.*
*The valleys deck themselves with grain.*
*They shout and sing together for joy.*

בָּרוּךְ אַתָּה יְיָ אֱלֹהֵינוּ מֶלֶךְ הָעוֹלָם מְבָרֵךְ הַשָּׁנִים.

*Barukh atah Adonai Eloheinu melekh ha'olam,*
*m'varekh hashanim.*

Blessed is God, for blessing our years.[11]

*Afterthoughts*

# At a Kibbutz in the Negev

Clear a road in the desert for Adonai.
Level a highway in the wilderness for our God.

—Isaiah 40:3

## Anticipation

> Tragedy is a soul without a body, and comedy, a
> body without a soul. King Lear in the forest, who
> used to have a body: throne, followers, scepter, a red
> robe on his shoulders and a crown on his head, and
> lost that body—he is tragic. And on the other hand,
> when the clown comes on stage and puts on a body
> royal, but inside, remains what he was—this is com-
> edy. So far we have been tragedy, an abstract soul
> without a body. And the state—this is the form, the
> body we put on.

So spoke David Ben-Gurion, who spoke also for others of his generation who understood the need for a Jewish
"body": ordinary men and women who would work the
ground, develop industry, vote for a government, and walk
the streets of cities and of towns, free and unafraid.

So much of Israel is now so built up that it is hard to
recognize what a miracle it all once was. It is hard to believe
that there once were swamps in the Galil, that Tel Aviv was
only sand dunes, or that Jerusalem was a dusty colonial out-
post ravaged by filth and disease.

But the desert still speaks of a miracle in the making.
Stand just a mile or two outside the settlements and you
understand immediately why everyone said, "You cannot
settle people in the Negev." But we did. And we still are.
The bulk of the land is still what it has been for centuries:
unwatered wasteland, pure wilderness where sandstorms
rage, where no water falls, and where the best you can expect
is a *chamsin*, a wind so saturated with heat it blows the desert

dryness all the way to Jerusalem and Tel Aviv. But here and there, the settlements stand out, magnets of opportunity for those still bold enough to pioneer a future.

## *Approach*

Psalm 126

שִׁיר הַמַּעֲלוֹת,
בְּשׁוּב יְיָ אֶת שִׁיבַת צִיּוֹן
הָיִינוּ כְּחֹלְמִים.
אָז יִמָּלֵא שְׂחוֹק פִּינוּ
וּלְשׁוֹנֵנוּ רִנָּה,
אָז יֹאמְרוּ בַגּוֹיִם
הִגְדִּיל יְיָ לַעֲשׂוֹת עִם אֵלֶּה.
הִגְדִּיל יְיָ לַעֲשׂוֹת עִמָּנוּ
הָיִינוּ שְׂמֵחִים.

*A song of ascents . . .*
*When our God brought back those who returned to*
*    Zion,*
*We were like dreamers.*
*Our mouth was filled with laughter*
*Our tongues with shouts of joy.*
*Among the nations, people said,*
*"Adonai has done great things for these people."*
*Adonai has done great things with us,*
*and we rejoice.*

*Restore our fortunes, O God,*
*Like the watercourses of the Negev.*
*May those who sow in tears*
*Reap with shouts of joy. . . .*
*Bringing in their sheaves.*

(If you have an opportunity to eat at the kibbutz, see special prayers for the occasion, p. 215.)

## *Acknowledgment*

(To be said in the fields of the kibbutz, looking out toward the desert round about it.)

Psalm 107:35–37

יָשֵׂם מִדְבָּר לַאֲגַם מַיִם
וְאֶרֶץ צִיָּה לְמֹצָאֵי מָיִם:
וַיּוֹשֶׁב שָׁם רְעֵבִים
וַיְכוֹנְנוּ עִיר מוֹשָׁב:
וַיִּזְרְעוּ שָׂדוֹת וַיִּטְּעוּ כְרָמִים וַיַּעֲשׂוּ פְּרִי תְבוּאָה:

God turns the desert into pools of water,
The parched land into springs of water.
And there, God lets the hungry live;
They establish a town to live in.
They sow fields, plant vineyards, and get a fruitful
    field.

בָּרוּךְ אַתָּה יְיָ אֱלֹהֵינוּ מֶלֶךְ הָעוֹלָם קוֹרֵא בַּמִּדְבָּר.

*Barukh atah Adonai Eloheinu melekh ha'olam,*
*korei bamidbar.*

Blessed is God, who calls out in the desert.[12]

*Afterthoughts*

# Sedeh Boker—
# David Ben-Gurion's Home

I will again set up the fallen booth of David . . .
I will restore my people Israel.

*—Amos 9:11, 14*

The Jewish nation is going through a revolution.
We shall not return to what we were.

*—David Ben-Gurion*

## Anticipation

"You cannot buy a commonwealth; you cannot conquer a commonwealth. You have to create it by your own work. We don't want to say that this is our country because we conquered it, but because we made it, we remade it, we created it." So argued David Ben-Gurion, in a speech that he described as his most representative address, his finest hour. It was delivered in 1946 as an impassioned appeal to the Anglo-American Committee that threatened to keep even survivors of Hitler's camps out of Israel.

It might equally have served as Ben-Gurion's own epitaph, since no one more than he "made" the State of Israel, then frequently "remade it," and finally "created it" into the democratic republic we know today.

Born in Russia in 1886, he eventually settled in the Negev, a fitting place for a man who epitomized toughness, vision and endurance. It was Ben-Gurion who insisted on declaring the State of Israel immediately upon the termination of the British mandate. It was he who became the first prime minister; who directed the War of Independence; who declared Jerusalem to be Israel's capital. It was he who demanded and exemplified the Jewish state when most of the world opposed it, and many less courageous Jewish souls were afraid to risk it.

To visit his home in the heart of the Negev is to return to a time when the ovens of Auschwitz had barely cooled, the world's powers jockeyed for their own advantage, and this single-minded leader acted on a promise he had made to a conference of Jewish survivors at Bergen–Belsen, "We shall not rest until every one of you who so desires joins us in the land of Israel to build a Jewish state."

## Approach

### David Ben-Gurion: Statement to the Anglo-American Committee, 1946

I realize the intellectual difficulty of our case. There is no precedent for the history of the Jewish People and there is no parallel to the fate of this country, no precedent for the special significance this country has for us. There is no parallel to the relations between our People and this country. It is unique. People usually think in analogies and when they are faced with a new phenomenon, they prefer to deny the existence of what they do not understand. But it remains a fact, nevertheless. You have the unique case of the homeless Jewish People and their historic country.

One reason why Jews came over here is love of Zion, a deep passionate love, strong as death. There is no parallel to that in all of human history. It is unique but it is a fact. You will see it here. There are 600,000 of us here because of that deep undying love of Zion.

What is the source of this love? A man may change many things, even his religion, even his wife, even his name. There is one thing which a man cannot change, his parents. The parents of our People are this country. It is unique, but there it is.

More than 300 years ago, a ship by the name of the *Mayflower* left Plymouth for the New World. It was a great event in American and English history. I wonder how many people know exactly the date when that ship left Plymouth, how many people were on that ship, and what kind of bread those people ate when they left Plymouth.

Well, more than 3,300 years ago, the Jews left Egypt. It was more than 3,000 years before the *Mayflower*, and every Jew in the world knows exactly the date when we left. It was on the fifteenth day of Nisan. The bread they ate was *matzah*. Up to this very day, all the Jews in the world on the fifteenth day of Nisan eat the same *matzah* and tell the story of the exile in Egypt. They tell what happened, and finish with these two sentences: "This year we were slaves; next year we shall be free. This year we are here; next year we shall be in the Land of Israel."[13]

## Acknowledgment

בָּרוּךְ אַתָּה יְיָ אֱלֹהֵי דָוִד.

*Barukh atah Adonai, Elohei david.*

Blessed is God, the God of David.[14]

## Afterthoughts

# Masada

*Masada must not fall again.*

—From the statement of purpose, sworn on Masada
by Israeli armed forces.

## Anticipation

All the world now knows about Masada, the mighty fortress in the Judean desert outfitted by King Herod between the years 37 and 31 B.C.E. as his palace; then the site of the last resistance and ultimate suicide of the Zealots, who had fled the Jerusalem siege by Rome in 73 C.E. It reached symbolic prominence in a poem by Yitzchak Lamdan, published in 1927. He spoke for the generation of pioneers risking self-sacrifice in their homeland rather than replicate endlessly the plight of defenseless Jews in eastern Europe. The hero of the poem is a pioneer who affirms, "I was sent by my people and will endure any hardship for them. The God of Masada is 'the God of the brave few.'"

By the 1960s, Masada was fully excavated, and immediately captured the Jewish imagination despite the troubling theme of the Jews who committed suicide rather than face capture by the Romans. Year after year, recruits to the armed forces climbed its snake path as the final leg of a desert march that lasted two days and two nights. After changing clothes, they would regroup in formal parade formation for a torch-light swearing-in ceremony during which each recruit would receive a weapon and a Bible.

On December 15, 1986, the swearing-in ceremony atop Masada was abandoned. Its underlying message of heroes who commit suicide no longer captured the imagination of a Jewish state which emphasized life, not death, and victory rather than defeat. But the ideal of military self-sufficiency and the need to remain firm in the commitment to Israel's defense remains as much a part of Israeli culture as ever.

# *Approach*

### The speech by Eliezer, leader at Masada.
### From *Wars of the Jews*, Flavius Josephus

Since we, long ago, my generous friends, resolved never to be servants to the Romans, nor to give obedience to any other than God, who alone is the true and just master of humanity, the time has come obliging us to make that resolution true in practice. Let us not at this time bring a reproach upon ourselves for self-contradiction. If formerly we would not undergo slavery, must we now choose such intolerable punishments? This will occur if the Romans take power over us while we still live. We were the very first to revolt against them.

I cannot but deem it a favor that God has granted us, that we still have the power to die bravely and in a state of freedom—which has not been the case with others who were conquered unexpectedly. It is very plain that we shall be taken within a day's time; but it is still possible to die gloriously together with our dearest friends. This is what our enemies themselves cannot by any means prevent, although they want to take us alive. We simply cannot still propose that we fight them off and beat them.

To be sure, we dimly hoped to preserve ourselves still in a state of freedom, as we had been guilty of no sins ourselves against God, nor been partner to the sins of others. We also taught others to preserve their liberty. But consider how God has convinced us that our hopes were in vain, by bringing upon us the distress of the desperate state in which we now find ourselves. It is beyond anything we might have anticipated, since the nature of this fortress, in itself unconquerable, has not proved a means for our deliverance. Even though we still have food in great abundance and a vast quantity (more than we want) of arms and other necessities, we are openly deprived by God of all hope of deliverance.

This was the result of God's anger against us for our many sins of which we are guilty in a most extravagant and insolent way, with regard to our fellow citizens; the punishment for which let us not receive from the Romans, but from God, as executed by our own hands, for the latter will be more moderate than the former. Let our wives die before they are raped, and our children before they have tasted slavery; and after we have slain them, let us bestow that glorious benefit upon one another mutually, and preserve ourselves in freedom, as an excellent funeral memorial to ourselves.

But first, let us destroy our money and the fortress, by fire, for I am well assured that the Romans will be greatly saddened to find themselves unable to seize our bodies and our wealth as well. Let us spare nothing but our provisions, for they will be a testimonial when we are dead that we were not subdued for want of necessities, but that, in keeping with our original resolution, we have preferred death to slavery.

## Acknowledgment

(To be said, perhaps, in the synagogue atop Masada.)

בְּיָדוֹ אַפְקִיד רוּחִי, בְּעֵת אִישַׁן וְאָעִירָה.
וְעִם רוּחִי גְּוִיָּתִי, יְיָ לִי וְלֹא אִירָא.
בָּרוּךְ אַתָּה יְיָ אֱלֹהֵינוּ מֶלֶךְ הָעוֹלָם
שׁוֹמֵר עַמּוֹ יִשְׂרָאֵל לָעַד.

*B'yado afkid ruchi b'eit ishan v'a'ira,*
*V'im ruchi g'viyati; Adonai li v'lo ira*
*Barukh atah Adonai Eloheinu melekh ha'olam,*
*shomer amo yisra'el la'ad*

I place my soul in God's care when I sleep and when I wake.
And with my soul, my body; God is with me; I do not fear.
Blessed is God who guards our people Israel forever.[15]

*Afterthoughts*

## This Place Is Holy

God said to Abram, "Raise your eyes
and look out from where you are,
*tsafonah v'negbah v'kedmah v'yamah,*
to the north and south, to the east and west,
for I give all the land that you see
to you and your ancestors forever."
—*Genesis 13:14–15*

# JERUSALEM AND VICINITY:
## *"Kedmah—to the East"*

# Allenby Bridge

It may be your destiny to be a bridge between Asia and
Europe. That, I firmly believe, is the mission of Zionism.

—*Sir Mark Sykes of the British Foreign Office,*
*addressing a mass meeting at the London Opera House*
*following the Balfour Declaration*

## Anticipation

On October 31, 1917, Lord Balfour announced Great
Britain's intention to establish a Jewish state. London's *Jewish
Chronicle* waxed eloquent over England, "The friend of our
people for generations. . . . Never was she truer to her noble
traditions than today—never more England than now!"

On December 2 British Jews gathered to celebrate Balfour's declaration. The eminent Lord Rothschild presided
and handed the microphone to Herbert Samuel, the cabinet member who had jockeyed for the bill behind the
scenes, and who now, for the first time, gave public expression to the arguments behind the Zionist dream. He concluded his remarks with the final line from the Haggadah,
*L'shanah haba'ah birushalayim,* "Next year in Jerusalem." Chief
Rabbi Hertz recited Psalm 126, "When our God brought
back those who returned to Zion, we were like dreamers,"
and reminded the people that many centuries ago, another
set of exiles (living in Babylonia) had gone home. Rabbi
Moses Gaster, a scholar and leader of the British Sefardi
community, followed, recalling an old legend that when the
Temple fell, bits of its masonry lodged in the heart of every
Jew. Gaster concluded, "I feel the stone in my heart already
loosening."

Jews throughout the world waited anxiously to see if
Britain would make good on its promise. Then, one day,
their attention was drawn to a tiny bridge named for General Edmund Allenby, no Zionist sympathizer himself, but a

loyal soldier at war with Turkey, and anxious to build a base of operations in Palestine. His troops attacked Jerusalem from the east on November 18, and less than a month later, Jerusalem was in British hands. On December 11, Allenby (accompanied by General T. E. Lawrence, better known as Lawrence of Arabia) entered the city.

"It was a brilliant day," Allenby wrote home to his wife. "Hoar frost here, in the early A.M., and then iced sunshine, with no wind. We could see, from the top of the house, the mountains of Moab; deep blue and huge. The Dead Sea lay too low to be seen."

Allenby rode through the area outside the Old City's walls, and then dismounted to enter the Jaffa gate on foot, the first Christian to capture the city since the Crusaders. Muslim soldiers from India were already guarding the Dome of the Rock, and Jewish units would arrive in less than three months. It was, he said, "the supreme moment of the war."[16]

## *Approach*

### Declaration of General Allenby,
### December 11, 1917

To the inhabitants of Jerusalem the Blessed and to the people dwelling in the vicinity:

The defeat inflicted upon the troops of the Turks by the troops under my command has resulted in the occupation of your city by my forces. I therefore, here and now, declare it to be under martial law. . . .

Since your city is regarded with affection by the adherents of three of the great religions of mankind, and its soil has been consecrated by the prayers and pilgrimages of devout people of those three religions for many centuries, therefore do I make known to you that every sacred building, monument, holy spot, shrine, traditional site, endowment, pious bequest, or customary place of prayer, of whatsoever form of the three religions, will be maintained and protected according to the existing customs and beliefs of those to whose faith they are sacred.

## *Acknowledgment*

(To be recited after crossing the border into or out of Jordan, at the first available opportunity.)

כָּל הָעוֹלָם כֻּלּוֹ גֶּשֶׁר צַר מְאֹד.

*Kol ha'olam kulo gesher tsar m'od.*

The whole world is a narrow bridge.

מִן הַמֵּצַר קָרָאתִי יָהּ
עָנָנִי בַמֶּרְחַבְיָהּ

*Min hameitsar karati Yah*
*Anani vamerchavyah*

In a narrow place, I called to God.
God answered me with great expansiveness.

שִׁיר הַמַּעֲלוֹת,
בְּשׁוּב יְיָ אֶת שִׁיבַת צִיּוֹן
הָיִינוּ כְּחֹלְמִים.
אָז יִמָּלֵא שְׂחוֹק פִּינוּ
וּלְשׁוֹנֵנוּ רִנָּה,
אָז יֹאמְרוּ בַגּוֹיִם
הִגְדִּיל יְיָ לַעֲשׂוֹת עִם אֵלֶּה.
הִגְדִּיל יְיָ לַעֲשׂוֹת עִמָּנוּ
הָיִינוּ שְׂמֵחִים.

*Shir hama'alot*
*B'shuv Adonai et shivat tsiyon*
*hayinu k'cholmim*
*Az yimalei s'chok pinu*
*Ul'shoneinu rinah*
*Az yomru vagoyim*
*Higdil Adonai la'asot im eleh*
*Higdil Adonai la'asot imanu*
*Hayinu s'meikhim*

A song of ascents . . .
When our God brought back those who returned
    to Zion,

We were like dreamers.
Our mouth was filled with laughter
Our tongues with shouts of joy.
Among the nations, people said,
"Adonai has done great things for these people."
Adonai has done great things with us,
and we rejoice.[17]

בָּרוּךְ אַתָּה יְיָ אֱלֹהֵינוּ מֶלֶךְ הָעוֹלָם הָעֹנֶה בְּיוֹם צָרֵנוּ.

*Barukh atah Adonai Eloheinu melekh ha'olam,
ha'oneh b'yom tsareinu.*

Blessed is God, who answers in times of trouble.

*Afterthoughts*

# *At the Jaffa Gate*

Adonai loves the gates of Zion.

—*Psalm 87:2*

## *Anticipation*

There is something about a gate. Jacob thought the angels in his dream came from "The Gate of Heaven." Yom Kippur's final service is called *N'illah*, the "closing of the gates," in this case, the gates of the ancient temple that clanged shut when the service ended. Judaism imagines human life as a series of gates opening and closing, opportunities gained and lost, chapters of our biography begun or ended. Fittingly, Jerusalem is best known as a city with seven gates. Nothing can sufficiently prepare you for your entry into the Old City's gates, probably the Jaffa Gate, the gate through which most people first enter the city. For your Approach tomorrow we provide a poetic translation of Naomi Shemer's magnificent song *Y'rushalayim Shel Zahav,* and suggest that the night before entering the Old City, your group gather to sing it together. If you are alone, be sure to read it before you go to sleep.

All but the last stanza of the song was composed before 1967, when the old city was still in Jordanian hands. It reflected the barrenness of the Old City, bereft of a Jewish presence, and the blockade that prevented Jews from heading south around the city into the area of the Dead Sea, Jericho, and Hebron. But that very year, Jerusalem fell into Israeli hands, and was reopened for Jewish pilgrimage and settlement. A fourth and final verse was added to reflect the new situation and celebrate our return.

When you get to the Jaffa Gate, pause long enough to make a complete three-hundred-and-sixty-degree turn in the street, letting your eye take in as far as it can see in the space between the wall of the Old City and the new buildings that have gone up everywhere outside of it. Imagine what it was like when Jordanian guns, mounted on the Old City's walls, rained fire down into the abandoned square where you now stand. This place, which was a "no-man's land" separated on both sides by barbed wire, is now Jerusalem's dominant portal to its past, a place where everyone may enter in peace.

## Approach

No poem better records the transformation of the divided city into a unified Jerusalem, with the Old City its spiritual center. If you are traveling in a group, take the time to gather outside the gate or in your hotel before leaving to sing it together.

יְרוּשָׁלַיִם שֶׁל זָהָב,
וְשֶׁל נְחֹשֶׁת וְשֶׁל אוֹר,
הֲלֹא לְכָל שִׁירַיִךְ
אֲנִי כִּנּוֹר!

*Y'rushalayim shel zahav,*
*V'shel n'choshet v'shel or,*
*Halo l'khol shirayikh*
*Ani kinor*

*Y'rushalayim,* built of gold,
Built of copper, built of light,
For your songs, I'm a fiddler,
By day and by night

The fragrance of the scented pine trees,
The wine-clear mountain air,
Form winds that greet the nearing evening
To sounds of bells everywhere.
In trees and stones asleep, aslumber,
A captive of its dreams,
The Temple sits inside our city,
Alone and unredeemed.

*Y'rushalayim . . .*

The ancient cisterns without water,
An empty city square,
The Temple mount without its keepers,
A city lone and bare.
And through the rocks and through the caverns,
The winds of sorrow roar.
The path by Jericho's untread now,
Down to the Dead Sea shore.

*Y'rushalayim* . . .

Yet still today I sing your beauty,
Place crowns upon your walls,
I'm younger than your youngest child,
A poet meek and small.
But your name—a kiss of angels—
Burns fiery and bold.
I'll not forget *Y'rushalayim*,
Our city built of gold.

*Y'rushalayim* . . .

To ancient cisterns, to the city,
We have come back again.
From the Temple Mount the shofar heralds,
The name, "Jerusalem."
And through the rocks and through the caverns,
There shine a thousand suns.
The path by Jericho announces
Our journey's just begun.

# Acknowledgment

To be recited immediately after walking through the gate.

Psalm 122

שִׁיר הַמַּעֲלוֹת: לְדָוִד.
שָׂמַחְתִּי בְּאֹמְרִים לִי
בֵּית יְיָ נֵלֵךְ.

עֹמְדוֹת הָיוּ רַגְלֵינוּ
בִּשְׁעָרַיִךְ, יְרוּשָׁלָיִם
יְרוּשָׁלַיִם, הַבְּנוּיָה
כְּעִיר שֶׁחֻבְּרָה לָהּ יַחְדָּו
שֶׁשָּׁם עָלוּ שְׁבָטִים
שִׁבְטֵי יָהּ עֵדוּת לְיִשְׂרָאֵל,
לְהוֹדוֹת לְשֵׁם יְיָ.
כִּי שָׁמָּה יָשְׁבוּ כִסְאוֹת לְמִשְׁפָּט,
כִּסְאוֹת לְבֵית דָּוִיד.
שַׁאֲלוּ שְׁלוֹם יְרוּשָׁלָיִם
יִשְׁלָיוּ אֹהֲבָיִךְ.
יְהִי שָׁלוֹם בְּחֵילֵךְ,
שַׁלְוָה בְּאַרְמְנוֹתָיִךְ.
לְמַעַן אַחַי וְרֵעָי,
אֲדַבְּרָה נָּא שָׁלוֹם בָּךְ.
לְמַעַן בֵּית יְיָ אֱלֹהֵינוּ
אֲבַקְשָׁה טוֹב לָךְ.

I rejoiced when they said to me,
"Let us go to the house of Adonai."
Here we stand within your gates,
O Jerusalem . . .

Pray for the peace of Jerusalem.
May they who love you prosper.
Peace be within your walls,
And security within your towers.
For the sake of family and friends,
I will now say, "Peace be within you."
For the sake of the house of Adonai our God,
I will seek your good.

בָּרוּךְ אַתָּה יְיָ אֱלֹהֵינוּ מֶלֶךְ הָעוֹלָם
הַמַּחֲזִיר שְׁכִינָתוֹ לְצִיּוֹן

*Barukh atah Adonai Eloheinu melekh ha'olam,*
*hamachazir sh'khinato l'tsiyon.*

Blessed is God, present again in Zion.[18]

*Afterthoughts*

# In Old Jerusalem

Walk about Zion, go all around it, count its towers.
Consider well its ramparts, go through its citadels.
That you may tell the next generation,
"This is God."

—Psalm 48:13–14

## Anticipation

There are many ancient cities, but there is only one ancient Jerusalem. When you walk its streets, you rub shoulders with your own family's history. As you quickly discover, you are a pilgrim in time, not just in space. The minute you enter from the Jaffa Gate, for instance, you see on your right remnants of the homes from the days of the Maccabees, while tunnels recently excavated under the eastern Temple Mount take you back to civilizations that flourished here long before King David was even born.

Just short of the Wall, there is the Jewish Quarter of today where settlers make new history while bustling past barely noticed ruins of medieval synagogues. To the nearby north, Christians walk the route called the *Via Dolorosa*, the path that Jesus took on his way to the cross. On the other side of the *Kotel* Muslims kneel in prayer at the Dome of the Rock, the mosque that honors the place where Mohammed is said to have been spirited to heaven.

We Jews take time travel well back before either of those events, obviously, but we stop to capture memories of less distant eras also; and we bring more history than we take away, for we each bring stories of our own, as A. M. Klein, the Jewish "poet laureate" from Canada wrote:

> I lift my visor. Know me who I am. . . .
> To those that begat me
> This body is residence. Corpuscular,
> They dwell in my veins, they eavesdrop at my ear,
> They circle, as with Torahs, round my skull,

132

In exit and in entrance all day long pull
The latches of my heart, descend, and rise—
And there look generations through my eyes.[19]

You want to walk Jerusalem's streets to capture the profound religious truth that "there look generations through your eyes." Walk around the city walls perhaps; stop to see what your great grandparents could only dream about from far-off ghetto homes. Take back memories, but leave some there as well—as poet Yehuda Amichai did, in the poem he recited when first he entered old Jerusalem after the Six Day War, finding spiritual echoes in even an old Arab's shop. You will read his poem tomorrow, as you approach your Jerusalem walk through time.

## *Approach*

### *On Yom Kippur,* Yehuda Amichai

*On Yom Kippur in 1967, I put on my dark holiday suit*
*And went to the old city of Jerusalem.*
*I stood for a long time before the alcove of an old Arab's shop,*
*Not far from the gates of Shechem [Nablus], a shop*
*Of buttons and zippers and spools of thread*
*In every color; and of snaps and buckles.*
*A glorious light and a great many colors,*
*Like a holy ark with its doors ajar.*

*I told him in my heart that my father too*
*Had a shop of such threads and buttons.*
*I explained to him in my heart about all the tens of years*
*And the reasons and the circumstances because of which I am now here*
*And my father's shop is in ashes there, and he is buried here.*

*By the time I was finished, it was time for* N'illah.
*He too pulled down the shutter and locked the gate,*
*And I went back home with all the worshippers.*

## Acknowledgment

(To be said, perhaps, at one of the restored synagogues in
the Old City.)

בָּרוּךְ יְיָ מִצִּיוֹן
שֹׁכֵן יְרוּשָׁלָיִם.

*Barukh Adonai mitsiyon,*
*shochen y'rushalayim.*

From Zion, let God be blessed.
God who dwells in Jerusalem.[20]

## Afterthoughts

# Har Herzl

*If you will it, it is no dream.*

*—Theodor Herzl (1860–1904)*

## Anticipation

Har Herzl, the mountain on which Herzl's grave now stands, holds also the resting place of Israel's many heroes, military and ideological. There is much to move you here: Herzl's grave itself, for instance, which symbolizes the dream for which all those buried here gave their lives; the memorial to Yitzchak Rabin, cut down in 1995 at a peace rally by an assassin intent on "holy" war. These two great men are book-ends in time, both of them visionaries, one for landedness after centuries of Diaspora life, the other for peace when all he knew was chronic war.

Most people head directly to Rabin's grave but take the time to visit Herzl's tomb as well. Like Moses, who never actually set foot in the Promised Land, Herzl too died without seeing his dream come true. Though he envisioned modern Israel, he never saw it born.

The Torah records how Joseph came to Pharaoh after Jacob died, pleading, "My father made me swear, saying, 'I am about to die. Be sure to bury me in the grave which I made ready for myself in the Land of Canaan.' Now therefore, let me go up and bury my father" (Genesis 50:5). When Joseph himself lay dying, "He made the Israelites swear, saying, "When God has taken notice of you, carry my bones up from here"" (Genesis 50:25). God took notice of the Jewish People, and we brought Herzl's remains to rest here too. He therefore lies reburied in the center of what is truly one of the most peaceful and moving spots in all Jerusalem.

## *Approach*

---

### At Herzl's Grave
#### Opening entry in *The Complete Diaries of Theodor Herzl*[21]

Paris, around Pentecost, 1895. For some time past, I have been occupied with a work of infinite grandeur. At the moment I do not know if I shall carry it through. It looks like a mighty dream. But for days and weeks, it has possessed me beyond the limits of consciousness. It accompanies me wherever I go, hovers behind my ordinary talk, looks over my shoulder at my comically trivial journalistic work, disturbs me and intoxicates me.

It is still too early to surmise what will come of it, but my experience tells me that even as a dream it is something remarkable, and that I ought to write it down—if not as a reminder to humanity, then at least for my own delight and reflection in later years. And perhaps as something between these two possibilities—that is, as literature. If my conception is not translated into reality, at least out of my activity can come a novel.

Title: The Promised Land!

. . . . How I proceeded from the idea of writing a novel to a practical program is already a mystery to me, although it happened within a few weeks. It is in the realm of the unconscious.

Perhaps these ideas are not practical ones at all, and I am only making a laughing-stock of myself to the people with whom I talk about it seriously. Could I be a figure in my own novel?

### At Rabin's Grave

*"We've known each other fifty years,"*
*said Shimon Peres of Yitzchak Rabin.*
*"He never agreed to sing."*

*But sing he did, a song of peace,*
*His final legacy,*

*"Our bitter cries will not revive*
*the man whose candle is snuffed out,*
*The woman buried in the earth.*

*But let the sun shine through the flowers.*
*Do not look backward.*
*Don't just whisper prayers.*
*Sing out boldly songs of peace."*

*Hear his intimations of a messianic age,*
*The budding hope of better times*
*Plucked unripened from a world still raw with rage,*
*But pregnant with the taste of peace.*

## Acknowledgment

(To be said while standing directly before these grave sites.)

אֵל מָלֵא רַחֲמִים,
שׁוֹכֵן בַּמְּרוֹמִים,
הַמְצֵא מְנוּחָה נְכוֹנָה
תַּחַת כַּנְפֵי הַשְּׁכִינָה,
בְּמַעֲלוֹת קְדוֹשִׁים וּטְהוֹרִים כְּזֹהַר הָרָקִיעַ מַזְהִירִים,
אֶת נִשְׁמוֹת כָּל אֵלֶּה שֶׁהָלְכוּ לְעוֹלָמָם
בְּגַן עֵדֶן תְּהֵא מְנוּחָתָם.
לָכֵן בַּעַל הָרַחֲמִים יַסְתִּירֵם בְּסֵתֶר כְּנָפָיו לְעוֹלָמִים,
וְיִצְרוֹר בִּצְרוֹר הַחַיִּים אֶת נִשְׁמוֹתֵיהֶם,
יְיָ הוּא נַחֲלָתָם,
וְיָנוּחוּ בְשָׁלוֹם עַל מִשְׁכְּבוֹתֵיהֶם,
וְנֹאמַר אָמֵן.

*El malei rachamim*

*O God, full of compassion,*
*You who dwell on high,*
*Grant perfect rest beneath the shelter of your presence,*
*Among the holy and pure who shine like the*
*    brightness of the skies,*
*To those who gave their lives for our land and for*
*    our people.*
*May they repose in Paradise.*
*Bring them under the cover of your wings,*
*And let their souls be bound up in the bond of*
*    eternal life.*
*God, be their possession;*
*And let their repose be peaceful.*
*Amen.*[22]

*Afterthoughts*

_____

_____

_____

_____

_____

_____

_____

_____

_____

_____

_____

_____

_____

_____

_____

_____

_____

# At the Knesset

In that day,
I will set up again the fallen booth of David;
I will restore my people Israel;
I will plant them upon their soil, never more to be uprooted.

—*Amos 9:11, 14*

## Anticipation

Known most for its Chagall tapestries and its British-style raucous parliamentary proceedings, the Knesset yet has its spiritual and religious side. Physically, it dominates the landscape and displays the menorah which became Israel's symbolic link between old and new. Unlike the eight-branch variety used for Chanukah, this seven-branch sign of modern Israel was originally a fixture in the ancient Temple, regularly outfitted and lit by the *Kohanim*, the priests, of old. Traditional Jews avoid all three-dimensional copies of it, preferring to await the time when God rebuilds the ancient Temple with its original menorah intact. Seeing itself as a sacred center for modern Jews, the Jewish state replicated the ancient symbol as its official governmental image. Modern pilgrims can only imagine the thrill of receiving a letter from the British government in 1917, saying that Israel might some day be born; or standing near here in 1948, hearing the Declaration of Independence of the State of Israel being read. But at least we can imagine it by reading the historic letter from Britain's Lord Balfour, known ever after as the Balfour Declaration.

Foreign Office
November 2nd, 1917

Dear Lord Rothschild,
I have much pleasure in conveying to you, on behalf of His Majesty's Government, the following

declaration of sympathy with Jewish Zionist aspirations which has been submitted to and approved by the Cabinet.

"His Majesty's Government view with favour the establishment in Palestine of a national home for the Jewish people, and will use their best endeavours to facilitate the achievement of this object, it being clearly understood that nothing shall be done which may prejudice the civil and religious rights of existing non-Jewish communities in Palestine, or the rights and political status enjoyed by Jews in any other country."

I should be grateful if you would bring this declaration to the knowledge of the Zionist Federation.

Yours sincerely,
Arthur James Balfour

## *Approach*

### Declaration of the Establishment of the State of Israel[23]

*Eretz Yisrael* was the birthplace of the Jewish People. Here, their spiritual, religious and political identity was shaped. Here, they first attained to statehood, created cultural values of national and universal significance, and gave to the world the eternal Book of Books.

After being forcibly exiled from their land, the people kept faith with it throughout their dispersion and never ceased to pray and hope for their return to it, and for the restoration in it of their political freedom.

Impelled by this historic and traditional attachment, Jews strove in every successive generation to re-establish themselves in their ancient homeland. In recent decades they returned in their masses. Pioneers, *M'apilim*[24] and defenders, they made deserts bloom, revived the Hebrew language, built villages and towns, and created a thriving community, controlling its own economy and culture, loving peace but knowing how to defend itself, bringing the blessings of progress to all the country's inhabitants, and aspiring toward independent nationhood.

In the year 5657 (1897), at the summons of the spiritual father of the Jewish state, Theodor Herzl, the First Zionist Congress convened and proclaimed the right of the Jewish people to national rebirth in its own country.

The right was recognized in the Balfour Declaration of 2nd November, 1917, and reaffirmed in the mandate of the League of Nations, which, in particular, gave international sanction to the historic connection between the Jewish people and *Eretz Yisrael* and to the right of the Jewish people to rebuild its national home.

The catastrophe that recently befell the Jewish people—the massacre of millions of Jews in Europe—was another clear demonstration of the urgency of solving the problem of its homelessness by reestablishing in *Eretz Yisrael* the Jewish state which would open the gates of the homeland wide to every Jew and confer upon the Jewish people the state of a fully privileged member of the comity of nations.

Survivors of the Nazi Holocaust in Europe, as well as Jews from other parts of the world, continued to migrate to *Eretz Yisrael,* undaunted by difficulties, restrictions and dangers, and never ceased to assert their right to a life of dignity, freedom and honest toil in their national homeland.

In the Second World War, the Jewish community of this country contributed its full share to the struggle of the freedom- and peace-loving nations against the forces of the Nazi wickedness, and, by the blood of the soldiers and its war effort, gained the right to be reckoned among the peoples who founded the United Nations.

On the 29th November, 1947, The United Nations General Assembly passed a resolution calling for the establishment of a Jewish state in *Eretz Yisrael;* the General Assembly required the inhabitants of *Eretz Yisrael* to take such steps as were necessary on their part for the implementation of that resolution. This recognition by the United Nations of the right of the Jewish people to establish their state is irrevocable.

This right is the natural right of the Jewish people to be masters of their own fate, like all other nations, in their own sovereign state.

Accordingly, we, members of the People's Council representative of the Jewish community of *Eretz Yisrael* and of the Zionist Movement, are here assembled on the day of the termination of the British mandate over *Eretz Yisrael,* and, by virtue of our national and historic right, and on the strength of the resolution of the United Nations General Assembly, hereby declare the establishment of a Jewish state in *Eretz Yisrael,* to be known as the State of Israel.

We declare that, with effect from the moment of the termination of the Mandate, being tonight, the eve of the Sabbath, the 6th Iyar 5708 (15th May, 1948), until the establishment of the elected regular authorities of the State, in accordance with the constitution which shall be adopted by the elected Constituent Assembly, not later than the 1st October, 1948, the People's Council shall act as a provisional council of state, and its executive organ, the People's Administration, shall be the provisional government of the Jewish state to be called Israel.

The State of Israel will be open for Jewish immigration and for the ingathering of the exiles; it will foster the development of the country for the benefit of all inhabitants; it will be based on freedom, justice and peace as envisioned by the prophets of Israel; it will ensure complete equality of social and political rights to all inhabitants irrespective of religion, race or sex; it will guarantee freedom of religion, conscience, language, education and culture; it will safeguard the holy places of all religions; and it will be faithful to the principles of the charter of the United Nations.

The State of Israel is prepared to cooperate with the agencies and the representatives of the United Nations in implementing the resolution of the General Assembly of the 29th November 1947, and will take steps to implement the economic union of the whole of *Eretz Yisrael.*

We appeal to the United Nations to assist the Jewish people in the building-up of its State and to receive the State of Israel into the comity of nations.

We appeal—in the midst of the onslaught launched against us now for months—to the Arab inhabitants of the State of Israel to preserve peace and participate in the upbuilding of the State on the basis of full and equal citizenship and due representation in all the provisional institutions.

We extend our hand to all neighboring states and their peoples in an offer of peace and good neighborliness, and appeal to them to establish bonds of cooperation and mutual help with the sovereign Jewish people settled in its own land. The State of Israel is prepared to do its share in common effort for the advancement of the entire Middle East.

We appeal to the Jewish people throughout the Diaspora to rally round the Jews of *Eretz Yisrael* in the tasks of immigration and upbuilding and to stand by them in the great struggle for the realization of the age-old dream—the redemption of Israel.

## Acknowledgment

(To be said, perhaps, in front of the Knesset, facing the large seven-branch menorah (candelabra) that is Israel's official state symbol.)

*Avinu Shebashamayim*: Rock and Redeemer of the people Israel, bless the State of Israel, *reshit ts'michat ge'ulateinu*, the beginning of the dawn of our redemption. Shield it with your love; spread over it the shelter of your peace; send forth your light and truth to those who lead and judge it, and to those who hold elective office. Establish in them, through your presence, wise counsel, that they might walk in the way of justice, freedom and integrity. Strengthen the hands of those who guard our holy land. Let them inherit salvation and life. And give peace to the land, and perpetual joy to its inhabitants.

בָּרוּךְ אַתָּה יְיָ עֹשֶׂה שָׁלוֹם בִּמְרוֹמָיו
הוּא יַעֲשֶׂה שָׁלוֹם עָלֵינוּ וְעַל כָּל יִשְׂרָאֵל.

*Barukh atah Adonai, oseh shalom bimromav hu ya'aseh shalom aleinu ve'al kol yisra'el.*

Blessed is God, who makes peace on high, and will make peace on us and all of Israel.[25]

# Afterthoughts

# *The* Kotel *(The Wall)*

Know before whom you stand.

—*The Talmud*

## *Anticipation*

The world is filled with walls that matter, some of them monumental in size or symbolism. The world's finances are still best symbolized by Wall Street, once a real wall at the north end of Manhattan's early population center. For centuries, the Great Wall of China defended Chinese from "barbarians." The Berlin Wall best represented the divided world of the Cold War, and its destruction, brick by brick, is probably the most fitting picture of the end of the Cold War.

For Jews, there is only one wall, *The* Wall, as it is called, or the *Kotel* in Hebrew. This is short for *Kotel Ma'aravi*, the Western Wall, because it stands at the western boundary of the Temple Mount, where it was once the retaining wall for the Temple's foundation. All that is left of the entire ancient Temple complex is this single simple structure. Jews have prayed here for centuries, wedging prayers scribbled onto paper into the crevices of its stones. If you have prayers with you from the people back home—or your own, for that matter—make sure you bring them with you.

Bring also your dreams and hopes. The Wall is a busy, noisy place, filled with Jews from all the world and Jews who live in its very shadows, all of whom are there in great numbers on any given day, saying their prayers. But it can be a private place too. Stake out a spot to touch it, even kiss it, if you dare. And just for a moment, be alone with God, and think the thoughts of Abraham Joshua Heschel who stood where you do and later wrote, "The Wall . . . . The old Mother crying for all of us. Stubborn, loving, waiting for redemption."[26]

## *Approach*

(To be recited, perhaps, just outside the official area of the Wall, but in full view of it, ready to enter its precinct.)

### From *Jerusalem, June 1967*
### by Stanley F. Chyet

*Who'd have dared shape the thought?*
*That we would come again to this antique rubble,*
*And that some definition of ourselves would grope*
    *its way forth from these stones?*
*That there was a backbone to the body of our mem-*
    *ories,*
*And that we could trace our backbone here,*
*In this eroded rock?*
*That millennia would not rob us of the longing to*
    *stand here,*
*Precisely here,*
*And that sophistications would not free us of the*
    *need to exult here,*
*Just here,*
*By this bone of Jerusalem,*
*With the great horn filling our ears?*


## *Acknowledgment*

(To be recited with one hand resting on the wall.)

*The Wall is silent. For an instant, I am her tongue.*
*. . . O God, cleanse my lips, make me worthy to be*
*her tongue.* [27]

(If you brought prayers from home, insert them into the crevices of the wall.)

*Afterthoughts*

# The Temple Mount

In the days to come, the Holy One of Blessing
will hold a chorus for the righteous and will sit among them
in the Garden of Eden. They will point their fingers toward
Him, as it is said, "It will be said in that day: Behold, this is
our God for whom we waited that He might save us.
This is the Lord for whom we waited; we will be glad
and rejoice in His salvation (Isaiah 25:9)."

—*The Talmud* (Ta'anit *31a*)

## *Anticipation*

Above the *Kotel* is the actual plateau upon which the Temple
once stood. It is now home to the great Dome of the Rock
and the El Aqsa Mosque. This place's primal holiness cuts
through time and embodies the gulf of religious difference.

Controversy is not new here: not only between Jews
and Muslims, but among Jewish factions too. Strict Orthodox opinion forbids Jews from climbing the Temple Mount,
lest they unwittingly defile the place where sacrifices once
were offered. In fact, at the entrance to the pathway upward,
you will find a warning sign and even a self-appointed
guardian announcing that Jews are forbidden to proceed.

Though contemporary Orthodox authorities are rather
unified on the matter, as late as one hundred years ago, they
were split on the issue. It actually goes back to a twelfth-century debate between the famed Moses Maimonides and an
outstanding critic of his, the Provencal authority Abraham
ben David. Maimonides held that the destruction of the
Temple did not annul the sanctity of the spot on which it
stood. Ordinary Jews, therefore, should avoid standing in
places reserved only for priests *(kohanim)*, and even present-
day *kohanim* should not appear there since, among other
things, they cannot dress in the required priestly dress, the
details of which we no longer even know. Jews who are not
Orthodox generally side with Abraham ben David, who

argued that the sanctity of the mount came to an end when
the actual Temple and its altar were destroyed. They conclude that Jews may have access to the Temple Mount area as
long as they respect the aura of the sacred that still hovers
over it.

## Approach

(From the pilgrim psalm, to be recited just before walking
up the path to the Temple Mount.)

### From Psalm 24

לְדָוִד מִזְמוֹר.
לַיהוה הָאָרֶץ וּמְלוֹאָהּ
תֵּבֵל וְיֹשְׁבֵי בָהּ.
כִּי הוּא עַל יַמִּים יְסָדָהּ
וְעַל נְהָרוֹת יְכוֹנְנֶהָ.
מִי יַעֲלֶה בְהַר יהוה
וּמִי יָקוּם בִּמְקוֹם קָדְשׁוֹ?
נְקִי כַפַּיִם וּבַר לֵבָב
אֲשֶׁר לֹא נָשָׂא לַשָּׁוְא נַפְשִׁי
וְלֹא נִשְׁבַּע לְמִרְמָה.
יִשָּׂא בְרָכָה מֵאֵת יהוה
וּצְדָקָה מֵאֱלֹהֵי יִשְׁעוֹ.
זֶה דּוֹר דֹּרְשָׁיו
מְבַקְשֵׁי פָנֶיךָ יַעֲקֹב סֶלָה.

*The earth is Adonai's and the fullness thereof,*
*The world and they that dwell therein.*
*For God founded it upon the seas,*
*and established it upon the floods.*

*Who shall ascend the mountain of God?*
*Who shall stand in God's holy place?*
*Those who have clean hands and a pure heart,*
*Who do not take God's name in vain,*
*And do not swear deceitfully.*

*They will receive blessing from Adonai,*
*And justice from the God of their salvation*
*Such is the company of those who seek our God,*
*Who seek to greet the God of Jacob.*


## Acknowledgment

(To be recited on the Temple Mount, close by the Dome of the Rock, which is said to be the place where the actual Temple sacrifice once took place.)

*Our God and God of those who came before us:*
*May regard for us and memory of our ancestors rise*
     *before you,*
*With mindfulness of Jerusalem your holy city,*
*And heedfulness of your people, the House of Israel.*
     *for deliverance and for good,*
     *for grace, love, and mercy,*
     *for life and for peace*
       *On this day of our pilgrimage.*

*God remember us for good.*
*God visit us with blessing.*
*God save us for life.*[28]

בָּרוּךְ אַתָּה יְיָ אֱלֹהֵינוּ מֶלֶךְ הָעוֹלָם
שָׁאוֹתְךָ לְבַדְּךָ בְּיִרְאָה נַעֲבוֹד.

*Barukh atah Adonai Eloheinu melekh ha'olam,*
*she'ot'kha l'vad'kha b'yir'ah na'avod.*

Blessed is God, whom alone we serve in reverence.[29]

# Afterthoughts

# The Southern Wall to the Temple Mount

"A song of ascents: Those who trust in our God are like
Mt. Zion, which cannot be moved, so abides eternally.
Our God blesses you out of Zion"

—*Psalms 125:1, 134:3*

## Anticipation

You are about to retrace the steps taken by thousands of pilgrims when the Temple still stood. In an age without photographs, they would come from all over the Jewish world, barely able to imagine what the sight of the Temple would be like. After a journey of days, weeks, or even longer, however, they would climb the stairs leading to the southern wall of the Temple, where two giant gateways ushered them into the Temple precinct. The one to the right was the entrance; the one to the left, the exit.

From the top of the stairs the worshippers had a marvelous view of the city. In front, the southern wall of the Temple rose majestically before them. Behind, was the area called the Ophel, a steep slope heading back down into the Kidron Valley. To the west worshippers could see the lower city, where David once had ruled. Up above the thousand-year-old lower city, the upper city sat like a crown, sparkling with mansions and palaces. To the east was a spectacular view of the southern side of the Mount of Olives, where the sun baked down on the thickly gnarled trunks of olive trees.

Climbing up the southern staircase, our ancestors would traverse a walkway that actually sat upon the roofs of interconnecting stores that had been built underneath. They would have visited the stores the day before perhaps, purchasing livestock and fowl for sacrifices or otherwise doing what pilgrims do to this very day: changing money, sightseeing through the shops, and buying mementos to bring back home. During the pilgrimage festivals (Pesach, Shavuot, and Sukkot) the lucky ones—with money to rent lodging and foresight to arrive early—filled the inns and extra rooms of private homes that served as antiquity's bed and breakfast places. Vast masses, however, slept outside the city or in the public places under the clear and star-lit sky, thinking, perhaps, of the challenge and ensuing promise that God made to Abraham, "Go forth from your native land to the land that I will show you.... Look toward heaven and count the stars. So shall your offspring be" (Genesis 12:1; 15:5).

## Approach

For almost 2,000 years, this access to the Temple precinct was closed. The Temple was destroyed in 70 C.E., and after the Bar Kokhba Revolt in 135 C.E. the Roman emperor, Hadrian, turned the entire old city of Jerusalem into a center for pagan worship, banning Jews from even being here. Eventually the sands of time covered up the entry way, leaving only the western wall available to pilgrims.

But people remembered how Jewish hearts had yearned to be in just this place. Unable to climb the stairs in person, they dreamed of being here every time they prayed. Our sixteenth-century source of Jewish law, the *Shulchan Arukh,* encoded people's yearning this way:

> When rising for prayer outside the Land of Israel, it is customary to face eastward toward the Land and direct our thoughts toward Jerusalem, the Temple, and the Holy of Holies. People who live in the Land should face Jerusalem, and fix their thoughts on the Temple and the Holy of Holies. If they inhabit Jerusalem, they should face the Temple and direct their thoughts toward the Holy of Holies.

Only in our time has archeology cleared away the debris of centuries and allowed us modern pilgrims to do what our ancestors did: to ascend the Temple stairs and stand in the spot where Jews long ago said they met God most regularly, most certainly, and most profoundly. Who knows what meeting lies in wait for us as well?

## Acknowledgment

(To be recited while ascending the steps of the southern wall)

Psalm 122

שִׁיר הַמַּעֲלוֹת לְדָוִד
שָׂמַחְתִּי בְּאֹמְרִים לִי
בֵּית יְהוָה נֵלֵךְ :
עֹמְדוֹת הָיוּ רַגְלֵינוּ בִּשְׁעָרַיִךְ
יְרוּשָׁלָםִ :
יְרוּשָׁלַםִ הַבְּנוּיָה כְּעִיר שֶׁחֻבְּרָה-
לָּהּ יַחְדָּו :
שֶׁשָּׁם עָלוּ שְׁבָטִים
שִׁבְטֵי-יָהּ
עֵדוּת לְיִשְׂרָאֵל
לְהֹדוֹת לְשֵׁם יְהוָה :
כִּי שָׁמָּה | יָשְׁבוּ כִסְאוֹת לְמִשְׁפָּט
כִּסְאוֹת לְבֵית דָּוִיד :
שַׁאֲלוּ שְׁלוֹם יְרוּשָׁלָםִ
יִשְׁלָיוּ אֹהֲבָיִךְ :
יְהִי-שָׁלוֹם בְּחֵילֵךְ
שַׁלְוָה בְּאַרְמְנוֹתָיִךְ :
לְמַעַן אַחַי וְרֵעָי
אֲדַבְּרָה-נָּא שָׁלוֹם בָּךְ :
לְמַעַן בֵּית-יְהוָה אֱלֹהֵינוּ
אֲבַקְשָׁה טוֹב לָךְ :

*A Song of Ascents. Of David.*
*I rejoiced when they said to me,*
*"We are going to the house of our God."*
*Our feet stood inside your gates, O Jerusalem.*
*Jerusalem built up, a city knit together,*
*To which tribes would make pilgrimage,*
*    the tribes of our God,*
*        to praise God's name.*
*There the thrones of judgement stood,*
*    the thrones of the house of David.*
*Pray for the peace of Jerusalem;*
*"May those who love you know well-being.*
*May there be peace within your ramparts,*
*    well-being in your citadels.*
*On behalf of my family and my friends,*
*I invoke your inner peace."*

*Afterthoughts*

# Mount Scopus

I declare the Hebrew University opened.
—*Lord Balfour, 1925*

## Anticipation

When the War of Independence ended in 1949, Mount Scopus remained an island of Jewish settlement surrounded by
hostile Jordanian forces. It had been courageously defended, as its high ground, immediately east of Jerusalem, presented a military advantage. In addition, it had already
achieved international fame because of two institutions that
dominated its heights: the old Hadassah Hospital and
Hebrew University. Health and education were the much
sought-after goals of even the earliest settlers.

To the west, Mount Scopus provides the most spectacular view of old Jerusalem. Poet Yehudah Karni wrote, "I
saw Jerusalem from Mount Scopus, and she was perfect and
whole, little but limitless, contained but not contained." To
stand on Mount Scopus today is to experience the non-con-
tainment of the Jewish dream, and the limitless capacity of
the human soul: in one direction, the most advanced con-
cern for the life of medicine and the mind, and in the other,
the vast expanse of Jerusalem, alive with history and beauty.

## Approach

It is the midst of World War I in Germany. The father, a successful entrepreneur, ardently supports the Kaiser. His oldest
son, Werner, is a Marxist, jailed for fomenting anti-war activity. His younger son, Gershom, age 20, is a Zionist, who
helped Werner distribute peace pamphlets, and as a conse-
quence, returned home one day to find a special-delivery
eviction notice from his patriotic father. Gershom Scholem

would someday, singlehandedly, bring to the world's attention the wisdom of Jewish mysticism. One of young Gershom's early mentors was Martin Buber, and as an adult, he went for long walks with Nobel poet S.Y. Agnon and poet laureate Chaim Nachman Bialik. They all moved to Jerusalem eventually, and typified the Jewish intellectuals who walked the streets of Mount Scopus and created the Hebrew University in 1925.

"There was enormous hospitality," recalls Scholem. "Everyone visited everyone. When you went out, you left the house open. It did not occur to us that there might be a theft. There was, in fact, no stealing, but when we returned, someone was often lying in your bed—the friend of a friend who had been given our address and wanted to spend the night."

As for the university, he remembers the day in 1925 when it opened. "Lord Balfour, the author of the Balfour Declaration, as well as greats of the Zionist movement from Weizmann to Rabbi Kook to Bialik to Achad Ha'am, sat on the tribune of the amphitheater, which had been carved out of the rock of Mount Scopus only a short time previously. I can still picture the old magnificent looking Lord Balfour standing before the setting sun and delivering his eulogy of the Jewish People, its achievements in the past and its hopes in the future."

General Allenby, representing His Majesty's Government, later recalled, "We were in a precarious position in every way. Dr. Weizmann, however, made light of this. Within the hearing of gunshot, he laid the foundation for the university." And after he had done so, Weizmann remembered, "We sang *Hatikvah* and *God Save the King*. But no one seemed anxious to leave and we stood silent with bowed heads while the twilight deepened into night."[30]

## Acknowledgment

(To be recited or sung from atop Mt. Scopus, looking down on the Old City.)

*From Atop Mt. Scopus,* A. Hameiri

מֵעַל פִּסְגַּת הַר הַצּוֹפִים
אֶשְׁתַּחֲוֶה לָךְ אַפָּיִם.
מֵעַל פִּסְגַּת הַר הַצּוֹפִים
שָׁלוֹם לָךְ יְרוּשָׁלַיִם.
מֵאָה דּוֹרוֹת חָלַמְתִּי עָלַיִךְ
לִזְכּוֹת לִרְאוֹת בְּאוֹר פָּנַיִךְ.
יְרוּשָׁלַיִם, יְרוּשָׁלַיִם,
הָאִירִי פָּנַיִךְ לִבְנֵךְ.
יְרוּשָׁלַיִם, יְרוּשָׁלַיִם,
מֵחָרְבוֹתַיִךְ אֶבְנֵךְ.

*From atop Mt. Scopus,*
*I bow down to you, Jerusalem.*
*From atop Mt. Scopus,*
*Shalom to you, Jerusalem.*
*For one hundred generations, have I dreamed of*
    *you,*
*privileged to gaze upon the light of your counte-*
    *nance.*

*Jerusalem, Jerusalem, light up your face for your*
    *child.*
*Jerusalem, Jerusalem, from your ruins, I will rebuild*
    *you.*

בָּרוּךְ אַתָּה יְיָ אֱלֹהֵינוּ מֶלֶךְ הָעוֹלָם
שֶׁנָּתָן מֵחָכְמָתוֹ לְבָשָׂר וָדָם.

*Barukh atah Adonai Eloheinu melekh ha'olam,*
*shenatan meichokhmato l'vasar vadam.*

Blessed is God, for extending wisdom to human
beings.[31]

*Afterthoughts*

# The Valleys of Jerusalem

Yea though I walk through the valley
of the shadow of death,
I will fear no evil. . . .

—Psalm 23:4

## Anticipation

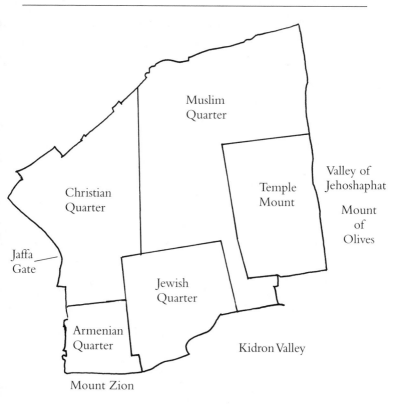

We normally think of the world's heights as a source of inspi-ration. But Jerusalem is surrounded by valleys, most of them famous, all of them moving beyond measure. Geography, like life itself, impresses us with its heights only if we know its depths. Take the Valley of Jehoshaphat that separates the

Mount of Olives from the Golden Gate at Jerusalem's east end. The prophet Joel exclaimed, "When I restore the fortunes of Judah and Jerusalem, I will gather all the nations and bring them into the Valley of Jehoshaphat" (Joel 4:1–2). And ever since then, it was assumed that the messianic era would be ushered in here. The most awesome is perhaps the extension of the Jehoshaphat Valley, the Valley of Kidron, where Absalom's tomb (among others going back centuries) is etched into the silent walls. And the most infamous is *Gehinom*, the Valley of Hinnom, where child sacrifice was practiced and whose name therefore became synonymous with Hell itself. No pilgrimage is complete without at least a short while spent in the depths of Jerusalem's valleys, knowing what prompted the psalmist in the depth of despair to say, "Out of the depths, I cry unto You, O God." But we should also realize what moved Ezekiel to see dead bones rising from the very bowels of the earth, perhaps the most well-known symbol of national resurrection and emblematic of Jewish hopes made real in Israel today.

## Approach

### From Ezekiel 37

The hand of the Lord came upon me. He took me out and set me down in the valley. It was full of bones. He led me all around them. There were very many of them spread over the valley and they were very dry.

He said to me, "O mortal, can these bones live again?"

I replied, "O Lord God, only You know."

And he said to me, "Prophesy over these bones and say to them, 'O dry bones, hear the word of the Lord! Thus said the Lord God to these bones: I will cause breath to enter you and you shall live again. I will lay sinews upon you and cover you with flesh and form skin over you. And I will put breath into you, and you shall live again. And you shall know that I am the Lord.'"

I prophesied as I had been commanded and while I was prophesying, suddenly there was a sound of rattling, and the bones came together, bone to matching bone. I looked and there were sinews on them, and flesh had grown, and skin had formed over them; but there was no breath in them.

Then He said to me, "Prophesy to the breath. Prophesy O mortal. Say to the breath, 'Thus said the Lord God: Come O breath from the four winds and breathe into these slain, that they may live again.'"

I prophesied as He had commanded me. The breath entered them, and they came to life and stood on their feet a vast multitude.

And He said to me, "O mortal, these bones are the whole house of Israel. They say, 'Our bones are dried up; our hope is gone; we are doomed.' Prophesy, therefore, and say to them, 'Thus said the Lord God: I am going to open your graves and lift you out of the graves, O my people, and bring you to the Land of Israel.'"

## Acknowledgment

(To be said while walking through one of Jerusalem's surrounding valleys.)

בָּרוּךְ אַתָּה יְיָ אֱלֹהֵינוּ מֶלֶךְ הָעוֹלָם
הַמַּחֲזִיר נְשָׁמוֹת לִפְגָרִים מֵתִים.

*Barukh atah Adonai Eloheinu melekh ha'olam, hamachazir n'shamot lif'garim meitim.*

Blessed is God, who restores souls to bodies already dead.[32]

*Afterthoughts*

# Yad Vashem

And Job . . . said, "Let the day perish
on which I was born . . . "

—Job 3:2–3

## Anticipation

On July 27, 1946, the Nuremberg Trials drew to a close.
Hitler, Himmler, Goebbels and several others who perpe-
trated the single most chilling mass murder in all of history
were all dead. But many were not: Hermann Goering had
served for a long time as Hitler's right-hand man; Wilhelm
Frick, the Minister of the Interior, had drafted Germany's
first anti-Semitic laws that had, bit by bit, stripped Jews of
civil rights and all means of employment. Hans Frank had
overseen the mass destruction of Polish Jewry; Alfred Rosen-
berg had masterminded the Nazi ideology of Jew-hatred;
Baldur von Schirach had orchestrated the indoctrination of
Hitler Youth; Fritz Saikel had overseen slave labor recruit-
ment. On the morning of July 27, Sir Hartley Shawcross rose
to conclude his trial summation for the prosecution.

He began with an eyewitness account of a mass exe-
cution by one of the *Einsatzgruppen*, the select commando
teams used to eradicate Jewish communities in towns overrun by the German army. Those in attendance had already
heard ten months of chilling testimony. Yet there could not
have been a dry eye even in that hardened audience, as
Shawcross described the murder of a thousand or more people—men, women and children—who were herded in
groups of twenty-five into a pit and systematically shot by
"an SS man who sat on the edge of the pit, a tommy gun
on his lap, and smoking a cigarette." The account described
some of the victims—ordinary folk, really—like a "father
holding the hand of a boy about ten years old and speaking
to him softly. The boy was fighting his tears. The father

pointed to the sky, stroked his head and seemed to explain something to him."

At the end Shawcross challenged the jury with these words:

> Mankind itself—struggling now to reestablish in all the countries of the world the common simple things—liberty, love, understanding—comes to this court and cries, "These are our laws, let them prevail!" You will remember when you come to give your decision the story of the mass execution, in a determination that these things shall not occur again. The father—you remember—pointed to the sky, and seemed to say something to his boy.

## Approach

A Dream, Yitzchak Katzenelson[33]

חֲלוֹם חָלַמְתִּי נוֹרָא מְאֹד —
אֵין עַמִּי, עַמִּי אֵינֶנּוּ עוֹד;
בִּצְעָקָה קַמְתִּי — אֲהָהּ! אֲהָהּ!
אֲשֶׁר חָלַמְתִּי, בָּא לִי, בָּא!
"הָהּ, אֵל בָּרָמָה!" אֶקְרָא רְתֵת:
"עַל מָה וְלָמָה עַמִּי מֵת?!
עַל מָה וְלָמָה מֵת לַשָּׁוְא?
לֹא בַּמִּלְחָמָה, לֹא בַּקְּרָב ...
נְעָרִים, זְקֵנִים, גַּם נָשִׁים וָטָף
כְּבָר אֵינָם, אֵינָם — סְפְּקוּ כָּף!"
כֹּה אֶבְךָ בִּיגוֹנִי, גַּם יוֹם, גַּם לֵיל —
עַל מָה רִבּוֹנִי? וְלָמָה אֵל?

*A dream I dreamt of terrible woe,*
*My people gone, alive no more.*
*I arose, with a shout: "Oh no!, Oh no!"*
*The dream I dreamt—It has become so!*
*"O God on high," shuddering, I cry,*
*"My people, dead! Wherefore and why?*
*Wherefore and why? In vain they died,*
*Not in war, fighting for their lives,*

*The young, the old, even wife and child,*
*They are no more—lament the sorrow!*
*All day, all night, I weep and cry,*
*Wherefore, O God? Why, Adonai?"*

## Acknowledgment

### A Service of Memorial for the Six Million

(The following set of prayers may be said alone or as part of a group. They are probably best recited in the Valley of Communities, near the memorial for a community that has some significance for people in the group. When the service is over, individuals may wish to find the marker for a community where members of their own family perished, and to repeat the two central memorial prayers below—*Yizkor* and *El malei rachamim*—at that spot.)

#### (Reader)

*We now testify to what once was,*
*And call to mind the people who died in a time*
*when evil walked the face of the earth.*
*They are no more.*

(In the following two memorial prayers, you may insert the names of any you know who perished in the *Shoah*.)

#### (Silent Meditation)

**Yizkor... *("May God remember...")***

יִזְכּוֹר אֱלֹהִים נִשְׁמוֹת יַקִּירַי ... שֶׁהָלְכוּ לְעוֹלָמָם.
אָנָּא תִּהְיֶינָה נַפְשׁוֹתֵיהֶם צְרוּרוֹת בִּצְרוֹר הַחַיִּים
וּתְהִי מְנוּחָתָם כָּבוֹד.
שׂבַע שְׂמָחוֹת אֶת פָּנֶיךָ,
נְעִימוֹת בִּימִינְךָ נֶצַח. אָמֵן.

*May God remember (my dear ones _____ )*
*and our brothers and sisters of the House of Israel*
*who gave their lives*
*for the sanctification of the divine name.*
*May they be at one with the One*

*who is life eternal.*
*May the beauty of their lives shine for evermore,*
*and may my life always bring honor to their memory.*

(Reader, or, if possible, chanted in the traditional manner)

**El malei rachamim . . .**
*("O God, full of compassion . . .")*

אֵל מָלֵא רַחֲמִים שׁוֹכֵן בַּמְּרוֹמַים,
הַמְצֵא מְנוּחָה נְכוֹנָה תַּחַת כַּנְפֵי הַשְּׁכִינָה
עִם קְדוֹשִׁים וּטְהוֹרִים
כְּזֹהַר הָרָקִיעַ מַזְהִירִים לְנִשְׁמוֹת יַקִּירֵינוּ שֶׁהָלְכוּ
לְעוֹלָמָם.
בַּעַל הָרַחֲמִים יַסְתִּירֵם בְּסֵתֶר כְּנָפָיו לְעוֹלָמִים,
וְיִצְרוֹר בִּצְרוֹר הַחַיִּים אֶת נִשְׁמוֹתֵיהֶם. יְיָ הוּא נַחֲלָתָם.
וְיָנוּחוּ בְשָׁלוֹם עַל מִשְׁכְּבוֹתֵיהֶם,
וְנֹאמַר: אָמֵן.

*O God full of compassion, eternal spirit of the uni-*
*verse,*
*grant perfect rest under the wings of your presence*
*to all our brothers and sisters who have entered eter-*
*nity.*
*Source of mercy: Let them find refuge for ever*
*in the shadow of your wings,*
*and let their souls be bound up in the bond of eter-*
*nal life.*
*The eternal God is their inheritance.*
*May they rest in peace;*
*And let us say: Amen.[34]*

(Reader)

*The memories of their shattered lives are woven in*
*our tapestry of history,*
*With blood-soaked reds and ghostly whites that will*
*not go away.*
*Sunrise yellow, autumn leaves, and deep blue skies*
*of every day*
*Must now compete for our attention.*

*Perhaps the colored blotches of our tortured past*
*will eventually fade,*

*Their threads run out.*
*Listen to Isaiah:*

(All together)

*Take comfort then, take comfort, O my people, says*
*your God. Speak tenderly to Jerusalem; proclaim to*
*her that her bondage is over, her iniquity pardoned.*
*She has received ample punishment.*

(Reader)

*We are the weavers now, entrusted with tomorrow's*
  *choice of wools.*
*Yellow can be sunflowers too—not just Auschwitz*
  *badges.*
*Sky-blue, blossom-pink, and Mediterranean-green:*
*that, I tell you, is the world that God created:*
*And that too is our history, just as much as chimney*
  *gray.*

*Let us leave this place sobered by our memories,*
*But thankful for today,*
*And hopeful for tomorrow.*

(All together)

*How greatly we are blessed.*
*How wondrous is our lot.*
*How beautiful our heritage.*[35]

*As every day for centuries,*
*We have celebrated life,*
*And declared God one.*

שְׁמַע יִשְׂרָאֵל יְיָ אֱלֹהֵינוּ יְיָ אֶחָד.

Sh'ma Yisrael Adonai Eloheinu Adonai Echad.

Hear O Israel, Adonai is our God, Adonai is one.

בָּרוּךְ אַתָּה יְיָ אֱלֹהֵינוּ מֶלֶךְ הָעוֹלָם זוֹכֵר הַנִּשְׁכָּחוֹת.

Barukh atah Adonai Eloheinu melekh ha'olam,
zokher hanishkakhot.

Blessed is God who remembers.[36]

## Afterthoughts

# Yemin Moshe (at The Windmill)

*From Moses to Moses, there was no one like Moses.*

—*Folklore*

## Anticipation

There have been many men named Moses in our history. At Yemin Moshe you will celebrate the memory of one of them: Moses Montefiore (1784–1885), possibly the most famous British Jew of all time. By the age of forty, he had made a fortune as one of only twelve "Jew brokers" (as they were known) in the city of London. He had also married into the Rothschild family. He devoted the rest of his life to Jewish causes, sparked in large part by something like a conversionary experience on his first visit to *Eretz Yisrael,* in 1827.

Though relatively unobservant as a Jew until then, he returned home to England on fire with Jewish commitment and spent the rest of his life as an Orthodox Jew. In 1840, he intervened on behalf of his own British government to save the lives of Jews in Damascus who were being charged with ritual murder. He was later knighted and named a baron for his humanitarian efforts on behalf of the Jewish People.

Sanitary conditions in old Jerusalem were deplorable at the time—with open sewers, unpaved streets, scattered garbage, and even dead animals lying decomposed along the dusty narrow roadways. British missionaries were establishing a hospital there which would take care of Jerusalem's Jewish population, while also introducing them to the Christian message. Jews had been trying to establish their own hospital as well. The most serious attempt, however, had been the initiative of Reform Rabbi Ludwig Phillipson, and when Jerusalem's Orthodox rabbis found out that he was Reform, they quashed the project. Montefiore, who was Orthodox, was able to revive the project under his own name. His plans were given a sudden boost when philanthropist Judah Touro of Newport, Rhode Island died, leaving $60,000 for his "unfortunate Jewish brethren in the Holy Land" and Montefiore as administrator.

In 1855, Montefiore made his fourth visit to Jerusalem, this time with money in his pocket to establish a hospital just outside the crowded city's walls. He hoped also to initiate a healthy rural agricultural settlement there. The hospital never materialized, partly because the French branch of the Rothschilds decided to build one on their own, and partly because of feuding among the Jerusalem rabbis. The agricultural effort died also. But his settlement remains, its very name, Yemin Moshe, "The Right Hand of Moses" (a reference borrowed from Isaiah 63:12), recalling its patron-founder. And the old windmill is still there, a charming memento of a time gone by.[37]

## Approach

### The Windmill in Yemin Moshe,
### Yehuda Amichai

This windmill never ground flour.
It ground holy air and Bialik's
Birds of longing, it ground
Words and ground time, it ground
Rain and even shells
But it never ground flour.

Now it's discovered us,
And grinds our lives day by day,
Making out of us the flour of peace,
Making out of us the bread of peace,
For the generation to come.

## Acknowledgment

(To be recited while standing in front of the windmill.)

בָּרוּךְ אַתָּה יְיָ אֱלֹהֵינוּ מֶלֶךְ הָעוֹלָם מַשִּׁיב הָרוּחַ.

Barukh atah Adonai Eloheinu melekh ha'olam, mashiv haru'ach.

Blessed is God who makes the wind blow.[38]

## Afterthoughts

# Mount Nebo

Who shall ascend the mountain of the Lord?

—*Psalm 29:3*

This refers to Moses, as it is said,
"And Moses went up to God" (Exodus 19:3).

—*Midrash to the last chapter of Deuteronomy*

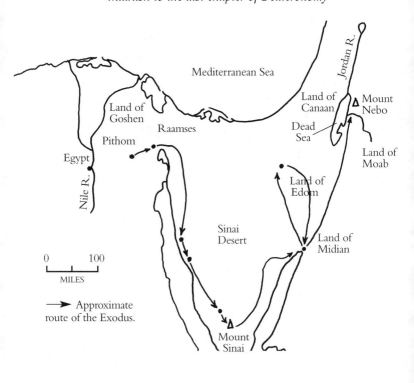

Approximate
route of the Exodus.

## Anticipation

The Israelites were never a sea people. When they left Egypt,
they could hardly embark on ships and cross the Mediterranean to one of the ports on Israel's western coast. But they
did not take the direct land route either, hugging the
Mediterranean's southern coast until they reached their destination. Our best guess is that after crossing the northern tip
of the Red Sea, they turned south and wandered the Sinai
desert for a proverbial forty years, then turned north again,

and entered Israel from the east through what is now the Kingdom of Jordan. Many biblical sites are therefore not in Israel at all, but in the land once populated by the Ammonites, Amorites, Moabites and other peoples through whose territory the Israelites passed on their way home. Of all these sites, the Bible recalls with special affection Mount Nebo. It was there that Moses died, after being granted his last look at the land to which he had faithfully led his people, but which he would never enter.

The midrash (Deuteronomy *Rabbah*) remembers his last minutes this way:

> Upon hearing of the decree that Moses would die without entering Israel, the angels objected, but in vain. God descended in person to do the deed, and said, "Moses, fold your eyelids over your eyes." And he did so. Then God said, "Place your hands upon your breast," and he did so. So God said, "Put your feet next to one another," and he did so.
>
> God then summoned Moses' soul, explaining, "You were assigned to Moses' body for 120 years. The time is up. You may now leave."
>
> But the soul objected, "You created me and You formed me; You breathed me into Moses' body for 120 years. All that is true. But could there be a purer body than that of Moses? I love him and do not want to leave."
>
> "Soul," God replied, "I will raise you to the highest heaven where you will occupy a place of special grandeur. Do not fear. But the time has come. You must leave."
>
> Still the soul resisted, saying one last time, "I beg of You, let me remain forever in the body of Moses."
>
> God saw and understood, but there was nothing God could do. Stooping low upon the bed where Moses lay, God gave Moses a kiss and took the soul away with a kiss. Then God wept, as did the heavens and the earth, and all the ministering angels. All of Israel joined the angels in mourning, saying, "He shall come to peace; those who walk in uprightness shall have rest" (Isaiah 57:2). "The memory of the righteous shall be a blessing" (Proverbs 10:7).

## Approach

*The Death of Moses* (Deuteronomy 34:1–12)

Moses went up from the steps of Moab to Mt. Nebo, to the summit of Pisgah, opposite Jericho, and the Lord showed him the whole land; Gilead as far as Dan; all of Naphtali; the land of Ephraim and Manasseh; the whole land of Judah as far as the Mediterranean; the Negev; and the plain—the Valley of Jericho, the city of palm trees—as far as Zoar. And the Lord said to him, "This is the land of which I swore to Abraham, Isaac and Jacob, I will give it to your offspring. I have let you see it with your own eyes, but you shall not cross there."

So Moses, the servant of the Lord, died there, in the land of Moab, at the command of the Lord. He buried him in the valley in the land of Moab, near Beth-Pe'or, and no one knows his burial place to this day. Moses was a hundred and twenty years old when he died; his eyes were undimmed and his vigor unabated. And the Israelites bewailed Moses in the steppes of Moab for thirty days.

The wailing period in the mourning of Moses came to an end. Now Joshua the son of Nun was filled with the spirit of wisdom because Moses had laid his hands on him; and the Israelites heeded him, doing as the Lord had commanded Moses.

Never again did there arise in Israel a prophet like Moses, whom the Lord singled out face to face, for the various signs and portents that the Lord sent him to display in the land of Egypt, against Pharaoh and all his courtiers and his whole country, and for all the great might and awesome power that Moses displayed before all Israel.

## Acknowledgment

*The righteousness which you have taught is
    eternal justice; your Torah is truth.
Your righteousness extends throughout the universe.
Your deeds reflect your greatness, incomparable God.*

*Your righteousness is like the lofty mountains; your*
*judgements like the great deep;*
*humankind and animals are in your care; help them*
*God.*

—*Psalms 119:142, 71:19, 36:7*[39]

בָּרוּךְ אַתָּה יְיָ דַּיַּן הָאֱמֶת.

*Barukh atah Adonai, dayyan ha'emet.*

Blessed is God, the true judge.[40]

*Afterthoughts*

# Hebron and Bethlehem: Tombs of the Matriarchs and Patriarchs

God of Abraham, God of Isaac, God of Jacob, God of Sarah,
God of Rebekah, God of Rachel, God of Leah. . . .

—*The daily liturgy:* Kol Haneshamah
*(the Reconstructionist prayer book)*

(At this writing, it is not clear whether it is possible or advisable to visit the sites where the Bible says our Matriarchs and Patriarchs are buried. Political considerations may make such a visit physically dangerous, and inadvisable from the perspective of Israel's relationship with its Arab neighbors. But in the hope that a secure and lasting peace will open Hebron and Bethlehem to Jewish pilgrimage, the following ritual is provided.)

## Anticipation

Jewish life before the descent into Egypt occurred very mainly in what is now the Arab territory east of Jerusalem. Only after the Exodus did the focus of our national destiny shift slowly westward to Jerusalem and the Mediterranean. "Home" for our bedouin-like forebears, from Abraham and Sarah to Jacob, Rachel and Leah, was likely a campsite in what is now the West Bank. If there had been a capital city at the time, it might have been Hebron or even Bethlehem, not Jerusalem. All but one of our earliest ancestors are buried in Hebron. The exception, Rachel, is buried in Bethlehem.

> Abraham buried Sarah his wife in the cave of the field of Machpelah facing Mamre, which is Hebron (Genesis 23:19).

> Rachel was in childbirth and had a hard labor. When her labor was at its hardest, the midwife said to her, "Have no fear, for it is another boy for you." As she was breathing her last—for she was dying—

she named him Ben Oni, but his father called him Benjamin. Thus Rachel died. She was buried on the road to Ephrat—now Bethlehem. Over her grave, Jacob set up a pillar; it is the pillar at Rachel's grave to this day (Genesis 35:16-20).

Jacob instructed his children, "I am about to die, Bury me with my fathers in the cave which is in the field of Ephron the Hittite, the cave which is in the field of Machpelah, facing Mamre, in the Land of Canaan, the field that Abraham bought from Ephron the Hittite for a burial site. There Abraham and his wife Sarah were buried; there Isaac and his wife Rebekah were buried; and there I buried Leah" (Genesis 49:29-33).

## *Approach*

Our Rabbis say that Jacob never died. Just his body lies inside the sepulcher, not his soul, for it is written, "Jacob was gathered to his people," not "Jacob died." Somehow his soul carried on, and still is felt like a tangible presence by us, his children, appropriately named *B'nai Yisrael*, Children of Israel, that is, "children of Jacob" whose other name was Israel, after all. His body gave out as he was blessing his twelve sons, the progenitors of the tribes of Israel, and therefore of us—as it is written, "Each according to his blessing, he blessed them." That means, say the Rabbis, that none of them received a blessing that was the same as the others; and so too, each of us is blessed in our own uniqueness. The way to know our blessing is to encounter the soul of Jacob, who will touch us softly as if with patriarch-hands, and whisper to us of our destiny.

Rachel too never really died, the Rabbis say, for it is written, "A cry is heard, wailing, bitter weeping, Rachel weeping for her children," to which God responds (anticipating Israel today), "They shall return. Your children shall return to their country" (Jeremiah 31:15). On their way to exile, Jews passed through Bethlehem to be embraced by Mother Rachel. So too with us; when estranged from all that is holy we know that Rachel our mother weeps for us, and rocks us gently in her arms.

From the tombs of our ancestors it is possible to feel the hands of Jacob and the arms of Rachel. It is possible to know with certainty that we are blessed and we are loved.

## Acknowledgment

(The grave site of matriarchs and patriarchs presents an opportunity to pray for blessing for those we love most. The following prayer provides a space to insert the name(s) of those for whom you wish to invoke blessing. It may be said in Hebrew or in English. If the one whom you wish to bless is present, it is appropriate to place your hands on his or her shoulders or head while saying the blessing.)

מִי שֶׁבֵּרַךְ אֲבוֹתֵינוּ אַבְרָהָם יִצְחָק וְיַעֲקֹב

וְאִמוֹתֵינוּ שָׂרָה רִבְקָה רָחֵל וְלֵאָה

הוּא יְבָרֵךְ אֶת _____.

*Mi sheberakh avoteinu avraham yitzchak v'ya'akov*

*V'imoteinu sarah, rivkah, rachel v'leah hu y'varekh et _____ .*

May the One who blessed Abraham, Isaac and Jacob,
Sarah Rebekah, Rachel and Leah,
Also bless _____.

*God grant (you/him/her/them) a long life, a peaceful life with goodness and blessing, sustenance and physical vitality, a life informed by purity and piety, a life free from shame and reproach, a life of abundance and honor, a life embracing piety and love of Torah, a life in which (your/his/her/their) heart's desires for goodness will be fulfilled.*

(You may pause and add your own words of blessing here.)

*Amen.*[41]

## Afterthoughts

# THE COASTAL PLAIN:
## *"Yamah—to the West"*

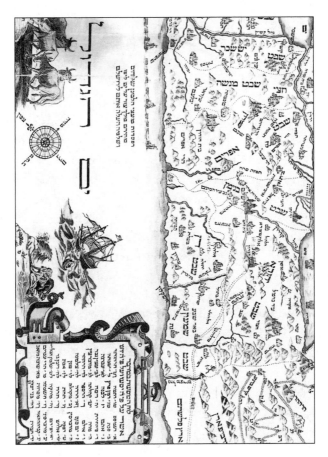

# The Mediterranean

The sea is God's; God made it.

—*Psalm 95:5*

## Anticipation

"In the beginning God created the heaven and the earth" (Genesis 1:1). That was Day One, some 4.5 *billion* years ago, the scientists say.

The "wild beasts of every kind" (Genesis 1:24) didn't arrive for another four billion years, and we humans are relative newcomers, born 2.5 million years ago. "God created man . . . male and female" (Genesis 1:27) but only when Day Six drew to an end. It took another 2 million years for those early human beings to look like us, and nearly half a million more for us to start counting "history."

By then our ancestors had discovered the Mediterranean. Abraham and Sarah got there from the East, about 2000 B.C.E. Joseph kept his brothers alive because as the mighty Nile River meets the Mediterranean, it forms a flood plain (like the Mississippi Delta) making food plentiful. By the year 975 B.C.E., King David had carved out a Jewish state, but to do so, he had to fight the Philistines, Mediterranean marauders whose ships set down on the shore of what is now the Gaza strip. Later still, the Mediterranean supported the navies of Alexander the Great and Julius Caesar. And just yesterday, as it were, the Islamic empire sailed its breadth and settled all of North Africa and even Spain.

Until 800 C.E., when Charlemagne developed European culture far away in land-locked France, most western men and women could not have imagined life outside the Mediterranean. At first, they had called it *Mare Nostrum,* Latin for "Our Sea." A third-century geographer named Solinus named it "Mediterranean"—"The Sea in the Middle of the Earth." Is it any wonder that the Rabbis recited a blessing for this sea of seas, the *Yam Hagadol,* or "Great Sea"?

Stand at the beach and watch the clear blue waves roll in much as people did when history first began. Our biblical author had this in mind when he remembered God saying on Day Two, "Let the water below the sky be gathered into one area" (Genesis 1:9).

Get there in time to watch the sun set, if you can, a pristine sight that hasn't changed since God said, "Let there be lights in the expanse of the sky" (Genesis 1:14). Some things are forever.

## Approach

*O God, My God*, Hannah Szenes

אֵלִי אֵלִי
שֶׁלֹא יִגָּמֵר לְעוֹלָם
הַחוֹל וְהַיָּם
רִשְׁרוּשׁ שֶׁל הַמַּיִם
בְּרַק הַשָּׁמַיִם תְּפִלַּת הָאָדָם.

*O God, my God,*
*I pray that these things never end:*
*The sand and the sea,*
*The rush of the waters,*
*The crash of the heaven,*
*the prayer of the heart.*

## Acknowledgment

בָּרוּךְ אַתָּה יְיָ אֱלֹהֵינוּ מֶלֶךְ הָעוֹלָם
שֶׁעָשָׂה אֶת הַיָּם הַגָּדוֹל.

*Barukh atah Adonai, Eloheinu melekh ha'olam,*
*she'asah et hayam hagadol.*

Blessed is God, who made the Great Sea.[42]

## Afterthoughts

# Haifa—Mount Carmel

The city of the future . . .

—*Theodor Herzl*

## Anticipation

Haifa is Israel's garden city. The road winds up from the beach through three levels of terraced dwellings, including "Carmel," named after the mountain on which the city rests. Its roots are ancient, prehistoric probably, but it has come into its own only in modern times as Israel's chief port. Still, the marks of history, old and new, are strikingly evident, especially in the city's southern approach from Tel Aviv. As the road curves around you see the mountain standing stark before you on the right; here Elijah fought the prophets of Ba'al, then fled King Ahab and Queen Jezebel, and journeyed south to the wilderness where he could hear "the still small voice" of God.

On the left is the remains of a ship (like the famous *Exodus*) which carried illegal immigrants (*M'apilim*) from Hitler's infernos, and then from post-war Displaced Persons camps, past watchful coast guards into British Palestine. The image of illegal ships breaking past the barricades runs deep in the older generation, not only here in Israel, but for all Jews alive at the time. Jews who survived the concentration camps were summarily interned once again behind barbed wire on Cyprus. By 1947, two full years after the liberation from Hitler, the Cyprus camps were full and getting fuller, to the point where a Passover Haggadah was issued in Tel Aviv for the detainees to use. On its cover was the image of the refugee ship, a promise of what was to come with Israeli independence in 1948: a final trip home, landing here in Haifa harbor, this time legally, with the spirit of Elijah looking down from Mount Carmel, as if the first steps toward messianic deliverance were really at hand.

Yehuda-Leib Cohen captures the flavor of the countryside where history and nature meet in mystical embrace, and where Elijah may not be the only spirit you encounter.

### *Upon My Death*, Yehuda-Leib Cohen

Upon my death—
Remember that I loved
The Carmel at sunset. . . .

Remember that I loved
plants sprouting through stones on a spring day,
and moonlit nights,
and playing in the waves on the shore
at the foot of the monastery
in the heat of the afternoon. . . .

Upon my death—
if my body falls into the hands of strangers
Please remember
and look for my spirit
in the Carmel. . . .

## *Approach*

### From 1 Kings 18

The word of God came to Elijah in the third year saying, "Go appear to Ahab. I will send rain upon the earth."

The famine was severe in Samaria, and Ahab summoned Obadiah who was in charge of the palace. (Obadiah was deeply in awe of God. When Jezebel was killing off the prophets of the Lord, Obadiah took a hundred prophets, hid them fifty to a cave, and provided them with bread and water.) Ahab said to Obadiah, "Go through the land to all the springs of water and all the wadis; perhaps we may find grass to keep the horses and the mules alive, and not lose some of the animals." They divided the land between them, Ahab going alone in one direction, and Obadiah by himself in the other.

Elijah met Obadiah on the way. When Obadiah

recognized him, he bowed low on the ground, and asked, "Is it you, my lord, Elijah?"

"It is I," he responded, "Go tell your lord that Elijah has arrived. . . ."

When Ahab saw Elijah, he asked, "Is it you, you troubler of Israel?"

He replied, "I have not troubled Israel, but you and your father's house have, for you have forsaken the commandments of Adonai, and followed Ba'al. Now, therefore, assemble all Israel for me at Mount Carmel, with the 450 prophets of Ba'al and the 400 prophets of Asherah, who eat at Jezebel's table."

So Ahab assembled the prophets at Mount Carmel, and Elijah said, "How long will you go limping between two opinions? If Adonai is God, follow Him; if Ba'al is God, follow him." The people would not answer.

Then Elijah said to the people, "I, yes, I alone, am left as a prophet of Adonai, and Ba'al's prophets number 450. Have two bulls brought for us. Let them choose one, dismember it, and lay it on the wood, but put no fire to it. I will prepare the other bull, lay it on the wood, and put no fire to it. Then you call on the name of your god, and I will call on Adonai. The one who answers by fire is God." "Well said," the people replied.

The prophets of Ba'al took their bull, prepared it, and called on the name of Ba'al from morning to noon, crying, "O Ba'al, answer us." But there was no voice and no response. They limped about the altar they had made, until at noon, Elijah taunted them, saying, "Cry loudly. Surely he is God. He may be meditating, or has wandered off, or is on a journey, or is asleep and must be wakened." So they cried aloud, as was their custom, and cut themselves with swords and lances until their blood gushed out all over them. As midday passed, they raved on, but still, there was no voice, no answer, no response at all. . . .

Then Elijah said, "Fill four jars with water and pour it on the offering and on the wood." Then he said, "Do it a second time," and they did. "Do it a third time," he said, and they did it a third time, so that water ran all around the altar and filled the surrounding trench also.

Elijah said, "O Lord, God of Abraham, Isaac and Israel, make it known today that you are God in Israel." Then the fire of the Lord came down and consumed the burnt offering, the wood, the stones, and the dust, and even consumed the water that was in the trench. . . .

Elijah said to Ahab, "Go up, eat and drink, for there is the sound of rushing rain." So Ahab went up to eat and drink, and Elijah went to the top of Carmel, where he bowed down on the ground, and put his face between his knees. He said to his servant, "Get up and look out toward the sea."

He went and looked, and said, "There is nothing."

"Go again," he said, "seven times."

At the seventh time, he said, "Look, a little cloud no bigger than a person's hand is rising from the sea. . . ."

In a little while, the heavens grew black with clouds and wind, and there was a heavy rain.

## Acknowledgment

(At the foot of Mount Carmel, facing the mountain and its caves where Elijah was said to abide:)

*May the Almighty again send us Elijah the prophet (may he be remembered for good). And may he bless each and every one of us in God's name. God grant us blessing, life and peace.*[43]

מִי שֶׁעָנָה אֶת אֵלִיָּהוּ בְּהַר הַכַּרְמֶל הוּא יַעֲנֶה אוֹתָנוּ.
בָּרוּךְ אַתָּה יְיָ אֱלֹהֵינוּ מֶלֶךְ הָעוֹלָם
מְשַׂמֵּחַ יִשְׂרָאֵל בְּאֵלִיָּהוּ הַנָּבִיא.

*Mi she'anah et eliyahu b'har hacarmel hu
ya'aneh otanu.*
*Barukh atah Adonai, Eloheinu melekh ha'olam,
m'samei'ach yisrael b'eliyahu hanavi.*

May the One who answered Elijah at Mount Carmel answer us.
Blessed is God, who gladdens Israel with Elijah the prophet.[44]

(At the *M'apilim* ship)

> *For any Jews, still handed over to persecution*
>     *or captivity,*
> *Whether they be stranded on land or on sea,*
> *May God show them mercy,*
> *And bring them out from the straits they are in*
> *To breathing space aplenty,*
> *From darkness to light,*
> *From servitude to freedom,*
> *Speedily and soon,*
> *And let us say,*
> *Amen.* [45]

בָּרוּךְ אַתָּה יְיָ אֱלֹהֵינוּ מֶלֶךְ הָעוֹלָם שׁוֹמֵעַ צְעָקָה.

*Barukh atah Adonai Eloheinu melekh ha'olam,*
*shomei'ah ts'akah.*

Blessed is God, who attends to calls for help. [46]

*Afterthoughts*

# Tel Aviv—Beit Hat'futsot (Museum of the Diaspora)

I came to the exiles of Tel Aviv, who lived by the river . . .

—Ezekiel 3:15

## Anticipation

> On Saturday, we would go out to survey the tract
> of land which stretched out before us with its gold-
> en sands while silence and emptiness were all about.
> We ourselves stood bewildered. How would a set-
> tlement arise on these shifting sands; how would
> houses be built and streets drawn? And indeed, there
> were skeptics who prophesied, "When hair grows
> on the palm of my hand, a suburb will arise on these
> sands. And even if you build houses here, the shifting
> sands carried from the seashore will soon cover
> them. You will always have to dig yourself out and
> protect yourself against the moving sands."

So wrote one of the original settlers, Rivka Alper, as she rec-
ollected Tel Aviv's origins. Once, this was nothing but sand
dunes, like the ones you cross on your way from the park-
ing lot to some of the beaches. But in 1909, visionaries came
here from Russia to do the impossible: to erect a city where
there wasn't even any water. They lived in crowded Jaffa,
next-door, and thought they were creating a tiny suburb
which they named *Achuzat Bayit*, meaning "Homestead."
As the city burgeoned, they sought a better name:

> Many meetings and discussions were devoted to this
> issue. Proposed were *Herzliah* (named after Herzl),
> New Jaffa, *Neve Jaffa* ("The beauty of Jaffa"), *Iriyah*
> ("Little City"), *Aviva* ("Spring"), *Yefefiyah* ("Beau-
> ty"), until Sheinkin (one of the settlers) revealed that
> a name had already been chosen for this place by
> the herald of the Jewish state himself—Herzl, in his
> book, *Altneuland* ("Old-New Land," Herzl's novel

about what a Jewish state would be like). Nachum Sokolow (Zionist thinker, author, and political leader after World War I) had translated it as Tel Aviv.

A *tel* is a mound of earth where antiquity lies buried. *Aviv*, meaning "springtime," connotes just the opposite: not yesterday but tomorrow; life renewed, not memories buried in the sand. Modern Tel Aviv is indeed these opposites: mostly the excitement of tomorrow, but here, at the Museum of the Diaspora, we recollect the past as well.

## Approach

*Poem Without End*, Yehuda Amichai

*Inside the brand-new museum*
*there's an old synagogue.*
*Inside the synagogue*
*is me.*
*Inside me*
*my heart.*
*Inside my heart*
*a museum.*
*Inside the museum*
*a synagogue,*
*inside it*
*me,*
*inside me*
*my heart,*
*inside my heart*
*a museum.*

## Acknowledgment

בָּרוּךְ אַתָּה יְיָ אֱלֹהֵינוּ מֶלֶךְ הָעוֹלָם
מְקַבֵּץ נִדְחֵי עַמּוֹ יִשְׂרָאֵל.

*Barukh atah Adonai Eloheinu melekh ha'olam,*
*m'kabetz nid'chei amo Yisrael.*

Blessed is God, who gathers together
the dispersed of the Jewish People.[47]

*Afterthoughts*

# The Guide to Blessing

*or*

## *How to Find Blessing Wherever You Go*

They shall plant vineyards and drink their wine.
They shall till gardens and eat their fruit.
I will plant them on their soil, nevermore to be
    uprooted,
From the soil I have given them—said Adonai
    your God.

—*Amos 9:14–15*

## For a Place of Aliyah Such As a Merkaz K'litah (Absorption Center)

וַתֹּאמֶר צִיּוֹן

עֲזָבַנִי יְיָ

וַאדֹנָי שְׁכֵחָנִי.

הֲתִשְׁכַּח אִשָּׁה עוּלָהּ מֵרַחֵם בֶּן בִּטְנָהּ?

גַּם אֵלֶּה תִשְׁכַּחְנָה

וְאָנֹכִי לֹא אֶשְׁכָּחֵךְ.

מִהֲרוּ בָּנָיִךְ

מְהָרְסַיִךְ וּמַחֲרִיבַיִךְ מִמֵּךְ יֵצֵאוּ.

שְׂאִי סָבִיב עֵינַיִךְ וּרְאִי

כֻּלָּם נִקְבְּצוּ בָאוּ לָךְ.

חַי אָנִי נְאֻם יְיָ כִּי כֻלָּם כָּעֲדִי תִלְבָּשִׁי

וּתְקַשְּׁרִים כַּכַּלָּה.

כִּי חָרְבֹתַיִךְ וְשֹׁמְמֹתַיִךְ

וְאֶרֶץ הֲרִסֻתֵךְ

כִּי עַתָּה תֵּצְרִי מִיּוֹשֵׁב וְרָחֲקוּ מְבַלְּעָיִךְ.

עוֹד יֹאמְרוּ בְאָזְנַיִךְ בְּנֵי שִׁכֻּלָיִךְ

צַר לִי הַמָּקוֹם גְּשָׁה לִּי וְאֵשֵׁבָה.

Isaiah 49: 14–15, 17–20

*Zion says,*
*"Adonai has forsaken me.*
*Adonai has forgotten me."*
*Can a woman forget her baby?*
*or disown the child of her womb?*
*Though even she might forget,*
*Your God could never forget you. . . .*

*Swiftly, your children arrive,*
*Look all around, and see,*
*They all assemble, they come to you. . . .*

*Soon you shall be crowded with settlers,*
*While destroyers stay far from you.*
*The children you thought you had lost*
*Shall yet say in your hearing,*
*"The place is too crowded for me.*
*Make room for me to settle."*

## The Law of Return

(Passed by the Knesset on July 5, 1950, marking the forty-sixth anniversary of Theodor Herzl's death. The law guarantees the right of every Jew to settle in Israel.)

Every Jew is entitled to immigrate to Israel. . . . The rights of a Jew according to this law . . . are transferred also to a child or grandchild of a Jew or to a spouse of a Jew and to a spouse of a child or grandchild of a Jew, but exclude a person who has willfully converted to another religion.

בָּרוּךְ אַתָּה יְיָ אֱלֹהֵינוּ מֶלֶךְ הָעוֹלָם
הַמּוֹלִיכֵנוּ קוֹמְמִיּוּת לְאַרְצֵנוּ.

*Barukh atah Adonai Eloheinu melekh ha'olam,*
*hamolicheinu kom'miyut l'artsenu.*

Blessed is God who leads us upright to our land.[1]

## *For a Place of Beauty*

*I Want Always to Have Eyes to See,* Natan Zach

*I want always to have eyes to see*
*The world's beauty; and to praise*
*This marvelous faultless splendor; to praise*
*The One who made it beautiful to praise,*
*And full, so very full, and beautiful.*
*I want never to be blind before*

*The world—so long as I am alive. I renounce*
*All other things, but never do I say "Enough*
*Of seeing this beauty in which I live,*
*And into which my hands extend like sailing ships*
*Plotting life's course. . . ."*

*I will never stop praising; my praise will have no*
   *end.*
*And when I fall, I will get up again—if only for a*
   *moment—let no one say,*
*"He fell!"—but, "He got up," for a moment, to*
   *praise*
*With eyes of hindsight*
*That for which praise should never cease.*

בָּרוּךְ אַתָּה יְיָ אֱלֹהֵינוּ מֶלֶךְ הָעוֹלָם שֶׁכָּכָה לוֹ בְּעוֹלָמוֹ.

*Barukh atah Adonai Eloheinu melekh ha'olam,*
*shekakhah lo b'olamo.*

Blessed is God, whose world is like this!

## For a Place of Blessing

(It is common at several places in Israel to request a blessing
for those we love, or to offer them such a blessing in person
if they are with us. The following prayer is recommended for
recitation at the graves of the matriarchs and patriarchs, but
may also be said at other, equally appropriate sites, such as
the Tomb of David in Jerusalem, or just at a Shabbat dinner,
wherever it may occur.)

*Mi sheberakh avraham yitzchak v'ya'akov*
*sarah, rivkah, rachel v'leah*
*hu y'varekh et _____ .*

May the One who blessed Abraham, Isaac and
   Jacob,
Sarah, Rebekah, Rachel and Leah,
Also bless _____ .

God grant (you/him/her/them) a long life, a peaceful life with goodness and blessing, sustenance and

physical vitality, a life informed by purity and
piety, a life free from shame and reproach, a life of
abundance and honor, a life embracing piety and
love of Torah, a life in which (your/his/her/their)
heart's desires for goodness will be fulfilled.

(You may pause and add your own words of blessing here.)

Amen.[2]


## For a Place of Miracle

From *Gates of Prayer*

*Days pass and the years vanish,*
*and we walk sightless among miracles.*
*God, fill our eyes with seeing*
*and our minds with knowing.*

*Help us to see,*
*wherever we gaze,*
*that the bush burns unconsumed.*
*And we,*
*clay touched by God,*
*will reach out for holiness,*
*and exclaim in wonder,*

*"How filled with awe is this place!"*

בָּרוּךְ אַתָּה יְיָ אֱלֹהֵינוּ מֶלֶךְ הָעוֹלָם
שֶׁעָשָׂה נִסִּים בַּמָּקוֹם הַזֶּה.

*Barukh atah Adonai Eloheinu melekh ha'olam,*
*she'asah nissim bamakom hazeh.*

Blessed is God, who performed miracles in this
place.[3]

## For a Place of Study

### If You Really Want to Know,
### Chaim Nachman Bialik

*If you really want to know the well*
*from which our martyred forebears drew*
*their strength of soul. . . .*

*If you really want to know the well*
*from which our oppressed forebears drew*
*God's comfort. . . .*

*If it is your fondest wish to see the breast*
*on which was poured a people's tears,*
*its heart- and soul-felt bitterness,*
*the place where cries broke out and gushed like*
    *water. . . .*

*If it is your fondest wish to know the*
    *all-compassionate*
*mother—aged, devoted, faithful—*
*whose full-embracing love collects her children's tears,*
*then wipes the eye that shed them,*
*then blankets her loved ones in the shade of*
    *stretched-out wings,*
*and rocks them to sleep on her knees. . . .*

*Tormented brothers and sisters,*
*If you do not know all this,*
*then. . . .*

*Turn to the synagogue, old and weathered.*
*To this day, you may see there*
*in the layers of shadowed darkness,*
*in some tiny corner, or before a wood-burning*
    *stove—*
*like skinny stocks of wheat, just a specter*
*of something long since come and gone—*
*Jews with faces shrunk and wrinkled*
*Golus Jews weighed down by exile,*
*Who, nonetheless,*
*Lose their cares*
*In a tattered page of Talmud*

*Or the age-old conversations of Midrash,*
*And wipe out worry by reciting psalms.*
*How desolate a sight this is to strangers*
*Who will never understand.*
*But your heart will tell you*
*That your feet tread the threshold of our House of*
*    Life,*
*Your eyes see the storehouse of our soul.*


מוֹדֶה אֲנִי לְפָנֶיךָ יְיָ אֱלֹהַי שֶׁשַּׂמְתָּ חֶלְקִי מִיוֹשְׁבֵי
בֵית הַמִּדְרָשׁ
וְלֹא שַׂמְתָּ חֶלְקִי מִיוֹשְׁבֵי קְרָנוֹת.
שֶׁאֲנִי מַשְׁכִּים וְהֵם מַשְׁכִּימִים,
אֲנִי מַשְׁכִּים לְדִבְרֵי תוֹרָה, וְהֵם מַשְׁכִּימִים
לִדְבָרִים בְּטֵלִים

*Modeh ani l'fanekha Adonai Elohai, shesamta*
*    chelki miyoshvei vet hamidrash, vlo samta*
*    chelki miyoshvei k'ranot.*
*She'ani mashkim vehem mashkimim.*
*Ani mashkim l'divrei torah vhem mashkimim*
*    lid'varim v'telim.*


בָּרוּךְ אַתָּה, יְיָ אֱלֹהֵינוּ, מֶלֶךְ הָעוֹלָם,
אֲשֶׁר קִדְּשָׁנוּ בְּמִצְוֹתָיו וְצִוָּנוּ לַעֲסוֹק בְּדִבְרֵי תוֹרָה.

*Barukh atah Adonai Eloheinu melekh ha'olam*
*asher kidshanu b'mitzvotav v'tzivanu la'asok*
*b'divrei torah.*

O my God, I thank you:
for giving me a place among those who sit in the
    house of study,
not among street-corner loiterers.
We both rise together at the break of day.
But I arise to words of Torah, and they arise to
    empty chatter.
Blessed is God, who commands us to study
    Torah.[4]

## On Praying in a Synagogue, New or Old

Jewish tradition remembers Balaam, hired by the king of Moab to curse the Israelites. Looking down upon the Jewish camp from a precipice on high, Balaam confessed:

> How can I damn whom God has not damned,
> How doom when Adonai has not doomed?
> Who can count the dust of Jacob,
> Number the dust-cloud of Israel?
> May I die the death of the upright,
> May my fate be like theirs.
> How lovely are your tents O Jacob,
> Your dwellings O Israel.[5]

By the Middle Ages, it became common to repeat an expanded version of Balaam's words when entering a synagogue to pray. Unlike Balaam, who could not count the Jews he saw, we do count ourselves, gathered for a *minyan*, and medieval Jews used the expansion of Balaam's prayer to do it. In the old manuscripts, the second Hebrew line sometimes appears in large type, reminding worshippers that it had exactly ten words. As the *minyan* gathered, its members recited the first line together, then used each of the following ten words to number off those in attendance. Today, the prayer remains with us still, a fitting meditation upon entering a synagogue, and a subtle recollection of God's blessing upon us. In just a few more years, Israel's population will outnumber the Jews of America, making Israel the population center of the Jewish People. "Who can count the dust of Jacob / Number the dust-cloud of Israel?"

When you are in Israel, you will surely want to attend a synagogue, joining your voice of prayer to those of our people who bring together liturgical traditions from the four corners of the earth.

When you go, say the traditional prayer from our Siddur, as follows, letting each of the ten words in the second line remind you of the blessing we enjoy, back home at last in the land of our ancestors.

(While outside the synagogue, say:)

מַה טֹבוּ אֹהָלֶיךָ יַעֲקֹב,
מִשְׁכְּנֹתֶיךָ יִשְׂרָאֵל.

*Mah tovu ohalekha ya'akov,*
*mishk'notekha Yisrael.*

How lovely are your tents, O Jacob, your
dwellings O Israel.

(As you walk through the synagogue doorway, say the following sentence, word by word.)

| | |
|---:|---:|
| *Va'ani* | וַאֲנִי |
| *b'rov* | בְּרֹב |
| *chasd'kha* | חַסְדְּךָ |
| *avo* | אָבֹא |
| *veitekha* | בֵיתֶךָ, |
| *eshtachaveh* | אֶשְׁתַּחֲוֶה |
| *el* | אֶל |
| *heikhal* | הֵיכַל |
| *kod'sh'kha* | קָדְשְׁךָ |
| *b'yiratekha* | בְּיִרְאָתֶךָ. |

*As for me, through your abundant mercy, I enter*
*your house.*
*In reverence before You, I bow at your sacred center.*[6]

(Find a place to sit, and continue . . .)

יְיָ, אָהַבְתִּי מְעוֹן בֵּיתֶךָ, וּמְקוֹם מִשְׁכַּן כְּבוֹדֶךָ.
וַאֲנִי אֶשְׁתַּחֲוֶה וְאֶכְרָעָה, אֶבְרְכָה לִפְנֵי יְיָ עֹשִׂי.
וַאֲנִי תְפִלָּתִי לְךָ, יְיָ, עֵת רָצוֹן;
אֱלֹהִים, בְּרָב חַסְדֶּךָ, עֲנֵנִי בֶּאֱמֶת יִשְׁעֶךָ.

O my God, I love your abode, the place where
your glory dwells.
I will bow and bend my knees, giving praise to
God, my maker.
Adonai, I offer You my prayer, at this fitting time.
God, in your abundant kindness, answer me with
your saving truth.

## For a Place of Recent Tragedy

*Every book should have a page it will not need
    some day,*
*Perforated at the margin for easy disposal,*
*Like a tear-off ticket to the world to come,*
*Or raffle chances you buy from scouts, local school
    boards, or the Heart Association,*
*Only this time, you get to win, not just save the
    stub in last year's files of things that never hap-
    pened.*
*When Elijah comes, he gets the page,*
*Testimony to the time that you put in, waiting,*
*When messianic hopes seemed dashed with every
    passing headline.*
*You were there.*

*Maybe the page is like those tickets that you used to
    buy*
*For trains that picked up passengers at every tiny
    crossing,*
*And you measured how far you had come by the
    number of punchholes*
*That your ticket had collected,*
*One for each unwanted stop along the way.*
*My Jewish ticket would be practically in shambles
    now,*
*So many punches through the years: Babi Yar,
    Terezin, the Munich Olympics. . . .*
*Elijah takes the ticket gently, folds it away at last,
    and says, You're finally home.*
*But keep the stub of course, to remember the train
    ride.*
*You were there.*

*This is the page my book would rather do without,*
*Punch-marked and perforated for past and future.*
*We pilgrim through time in the hope that our train
    will not stop*
*At yet another crossing where we'd rather not get
    out,*
*Praying that the page will soon be claimed at the
    end of the ride.*

*Or at least that the hardest part of the journey is*
*    over—*
*We'll skip over the page, no need to stop to have it*
*    punched again.*
*But if, perchance, there are a few more destinations*
*    to our destiny*
*Crossroads in time where once again*
*        some blood is spilled*
*        some laughter stilled,*
*        a single breath of life, needlessly cut off,*
*This page remains for somber presentation on the*
*    spot,*
*That you might know:*
*You were there.*

יִתְגַּדַּל וְיִתְקַדַּשׁ שְׁמֵהּ רַבָּא

*Yit-ga-dal v'yit-ka-dash sh'meih rabba*

*Mayence, Blois, York*

בְּעָלְמָא דִי בְרָא כִרְעוּתֵהּ
וְיַמְלִיךְ מַלְכוּתֵהּ

*b'al'ma di-vra khi-ru-tei v'yam-likh mal-khu-tei*

*Dachau, Buchenwald, Babi Yar*

בְּחַיֵּיכוֹן וּבְיוֹמֵיכוֹן וּבְחַיֵּי דְכָל בֵּית יִשְׂרָאֵל
בַּעֲגָלָא וּבִזְמַן קָרִיב וְאִמְרוּ אָמֵן.

*b'cha-yei-khon uv'yo-mei-khon*
*uv'cha-yei d'khol beit Yisrael*
*Ba'a-ga-la u-viz-man ka-riv v'im-ru amen!*

*Kishinev, Warsaw, Auschwitz*

יְהֵא שְׁמֵהּ רַבָּא מְבָרַךְ לְעָלַם וּלְעָלְמֵי עָלְמַיָּא.
יִתְבָּרַךְ וְיִשְׁתַּבַּח וְיִתְפָּאַר וְיִתְרוֹמַם
וְיִתְנַשֵּׂא וְיִתְהַדָּר וְיִתְעַלֶּה וְיִתְהַלָּל
שְׁמֵהּ דְּקֻדְשָׁא בְּרִיךְ הוּא

*Yehei shmeih rabba m'va-rakh*
*l'a-lam ul'al-mei al-maya*
*yit-ba-rakh v'yish-ta-bach v'yit-pa'ar*

*v'yit-ro-mam v'yit-na-sei*
*v'yit-ha-dar v'yit-a-leh v'yit-ha-lal*
*sh'meih d'kud-sha b'rikh hu*

*Treblinka, Chelmno, Bergen-Belsen*

לְעֵלָּא מִן כָּל בִּרְכָתָא וְשִׁירָתָא
תֻּשְׁבְּחָתָא וְנֶחֱמָתָא דַּאֲמִירָן בְּעָלְמָא
וְאִמְרוּ אָמֵן.

*L'ei-la min kol bir-kha-ta v'shi-ra-ta*
*tush-b'cha-ta v'ne-che-ma-ta*
*da'a-mi-ran b'al-ma*
*v'im-ru amen!*

*K'far Etzion, Munich, Ma'alot*
*Machaneh Yehudah, Ben Yehudah Street*

יְהֵא שְׁלָמָא רַבָּא מִן שְׁמַיָּא
וְחַיִּים עָלֵינוּ וְעַל כָּל יִשְׂרָאֵל
וְאִמְרוּ אָמֵן.

*Y'hei sh'lama rabba min sh'maya*
*v'cha-yim aleinu v'al kol yisrael*
*v'im-ru amen*

*(Add name of recent tragedy here)*

עֹשֶׂה שָׁלוֹם בִּמְרוֹמָיו
הוּא יַעֲשֶׂה שָׁלוֹם עָלֵינוּ וְעַל כָּל יִשְׂרָאֵל
וְאִמְרוּ אָמֵן.

*O-seh shalom bim-ro-mav hu ya'aseh shalom*
*alenu v'al kol yisrael, v'im-ru amen*[7]

*Let the glory of God be extolled, let God's great*
    *name be hallowed, in the world whose creation*
    *God willed. May God's dominion soon prevail,*
    *in our own day, our own lives, and the life of all*
    *Israel, and let us say: Amen.*
*Let God's great name be blessed for ever and ever.*
*Let the name of Holy Blessed One be glorified,*
    *exalted, and honored, though God is beyond all*
    *the praises, songs, and adorations that we can*
    *utter, and let us say: Amen.*

*For us and for all Israel, may the blessing of peace*
*and the promise of life come true, and let us say:*
*Amen.*

*May the One who causes peace to reign in the high*
*heavens let peace descend on us, and on all Israel,*
*and let us say: Amen.*[8]

## For a Place of Wisdom

Rabbi Yose Ben Kisma said:

Once, when I was walking along the way, I chanced upon a man who exchanged greetings with me. "Rabbi," he asked, "Where are you from?"

"From a large city of scholars and sages," I replied.

"Would you care to dwell with us, Rabbi?" he inquired. "I will make you a millionaire in gifts of cash and precious gems."

I responded, "Young man, were you to give me all the silver, gold, cash, and jewels in the entire world, I would never dwell anywhere but where there is Torah. When you die, you will be accompanied not by silver, gold, and precious stones but by Torah and good deeds alone, as it is written, 'It shall guide you when you walk, watch over you when you lie down, and be your subject for discussion, when you wake up' (Proverbs 6:22). 'It shall guide you when you walk,' in this world; it will 'watch over you when you lie down' in the grave; 'and be your subject for discussion, when you wake up'— in the world to come."

בָּרוּךְ אַתָּה, יְיָ אֱלֹהֵינוּ, מֶלֶךְ הָעוֹלָם,
שֶׁחָלַק מֵחָכְמָתוֹ לִירֵאָיו.

*Barukh atah Adonai Eloheinu melekh ha'olam*
*shechalak meichokhmato li'rei'av.*

**Blessed is God, who shares divine wisdom with those who are God-fearing.**[9]

## *For a Place of War*

*Lament,* Yehuda Amichai

The diameter of the bomb was thirty centimeters
  and the diameter of its destruction—
    about seven meters,
      and in it, four killed and eleven wounded.
        and around these, in a larger circle
          of pain and time, are scattered
            two hospitals and one cemetery,
              But the young woman
                who was buried in the place
                  from where she came, at a distance
                    of more than one hundred kilometers,
                      enlarges the circle considerably,
                        And the lonely man
                          who is mourning her death in a distant country
                            incorporates into the circle
                              the whole world. And I won't speak
                                of the cry of the orphans
                                  that reaches God's chair and from there
                                    makes the circle endless
                                      and godless.

אֲנִי מַבְטִיחַ לָךְ,
יַלְדָּה שֶׁלִּי קְטַנָּה,
שֶׁזּוֹ תִּהְיֶה
הַמִּלְחָמָה הָאַחֲרוֹנָה.

*Ani mavtiach lakh*
*yaldah sheli k'tanah*
*shezo*
*tihyeh*
*hamilchamah ha'acharonah.*

I promise you my child,
I vow with all my might,
That this will be the last,
The final war that we will fight.

בָּרוּךְ אַתָּה יְיָ אֱלֹהֵינוּ מֶלֶךְ הָעוֹלָם עֹשֶׂה הַשָּׁלוֹם.

*Barukh atah Adonai Eloheinu melekh ha'olam,*
*oseh hashalom.*

Blessed is God, who will bring peace.

## For a Place of Hope

*Hatikvah* (The national anthem of Israel)

כָּל עוֹד בַּלֵּבָב פְּנִימָה
נֶפֶשׁ יְהוּדִי הוֹמִיָּה,
וּלְפַאֲתֵי מִזְרָח קָדִימָה
עַיִן לְצִיּוֹן צוֹפִיָּה,
עוֹד לֹא אָבְדָה תִקְוָתֵנוּ
הַתִּקְוָה בַּת שְׁנוֹת אַלְפַּיִם,
לִהְיוֹת עַם חָפְשִׁי בְּאַרְצֵנוּ,
בְּאֶרֶץ צִיּוֹן וִירוּשָׁלַיִם.

*Kol od baleivav p'nimah*
*Nefesh y'hudi homiyah*
*Ul'fa'atei mizrach kadimah*
*Ayin l'tsiyon tsofiyah*

*Od lo av'da tikvateinu*
*Hatikvah bat shnot alpayim*
*Lihyot am chofshi b'artzeinu*
*B'eretz tsiyon viyerushalayim*

(Repeat last four lines)

As long as deep in the heart
A Jewish soul yearns,
And toward the East,
An eye looks to Zion,

Our hope is not yet lost—
The hope of 2,000 years:
To be a free people in our land,
The land of Zion and Jerusalem.[10]

בָּרוּךְ אַתָּה יְיָ מִקְוֵה יִשְׂרָאֵל.

*Barukh atah Adonai, mikveh Yisrael.*[11]

Blessed is God, the hope of Israel.

## For a Place of Muslim or Christian Worship

### *Maimonides,* Code of Jewish Law

Adam, the first man, was assigned six commandments: not to worship idols, not to take God's name in vain, not to murder, not to engage in forbidden sexual relations, not to steal, and to maintain courts to see that justice based on these laws was upheld. When Noah came along, a further commandment was given to non-Jews: not to eat meat torn from a living animal. All in all, then, God's covenant with non-Jews encompasses seven laws.

### The Talmud

Our Rabbis taught: we support the poor who are not Jewish along with those who are; we visit the sick who are not Jewish just as we do Jews; we bury the deceased who are not Jewish just as we do Jews—*mipnei darkhei shalom*—in the interests of peace.

בָּרוּךְ אַתָּה יְיָ הַמַּדְרִיכֵנוּ בְּדַרְכֵי שָׁלוֹם.

*Barukh atah Adonai, hamadrikheinu b'darkhei shalom.*

Blessed is God who sets our steps in the ways of peace.[12]

## For Seeing or Hearing Hebrew All around You

### *Hebrew,* Danny Siegel

*I'll tell you how much I love Hebrew:*
*Read me anything—*
    *Genesis*

*or an ad in an Israeli paper*
*and watch my face.*
*I will make half-sounds of ecstasy*
*and my smile will be so enormously sweet*
*you would think some angels were singing Psalms*
　　*or God Himself was reciting to me.*
*I am crazy for her Holiness*
　　*and each restaurant's menu in* Yerushalayim
　　*or Bialik poem*
*gives me peace no Dante or Milton or Goethe*
*could give.*
*I have heard Iliads of poetry,*
*Omar Khayyam in Farsi,*
*and Virgil sung as if the poet himself*
*were coaching the reader.*
*And they move me—*
*but not like*
*the train schedule from Haifa to Tel Aviv*
*or the choppy unsyntaxed note*
*from a student who got half the grammar I taught*
　　*him*
*all wrong*
*but remembered to write with Alefs and Zayins and*
　　*Shins.*
*That's the way I am.*
*I'd rather hear the weather report*
*on* Kol Yisrael
*than all the rhythms and music of Shakespeare.*

## For Planting a Tree

Before picking up the sapling, say:

> *Rabbi Yochanan ben Zakkai used to say: If you are*
> *holding a sapling in your hands, and someone*
> *announces the Messiah's arrival, plant the sapling,*
> *and after that, go meet the Messiah.* [13]

### The Tree and the Mashiach (*the Messiah*),
### Danny Siegel

No matter what reasonable people
or foaming enthusiastic youths tell you:
that this messiah or that messiah
is imminent—
plant!
The *Mashiach* is in no rush.
When you have planted down the last clods of
    dirt,
And watered your pines, your cedars,
your gum trees and cypresses,
he will still be wherever he is supposed to be,
and more than happy to admire the sapling with
    you.
Messiahs don't come to uproot things. . . .

Pick up the sapling and, while holding it in your hand, say:

*As my ancestors planted for me, I now plant for my*
    *descendants:*[14]

בָּרוּךְ אַתָּה יְיָ אֱלֹהֵינוּ מֶלֶךְ הָעוֹלָם
מַצְמִיחַ כָּל עֵץ חַיִּים.

*Barukh atah Adonai Eloheinu melekh ha'olam*
*matzmi'ach kol eits chayim.*

Blessed is God, who raises up each tree of life.[15]

## On Eating at a Kibbutz

You may have a chance either to eat a meal in a kibbutz or
to walk through the fields and orchards and pick some fruit
or produce. Tradition sees special merit in food grown in
the land of Israel, and we should, too, especially given the
modern miracle of making what was just desert or swampland blossom. The Rabbis provided special blessings for the
occasion.

**Upon picking fresh fruit or garden produce, say:**

כַּמָּה נָאָה תְּנוּבַת הַשָּׂדֶה זוֹ _____ .
בָּרוּךְ הַמָּקוֹם שֶׁבְּרָאָה.

*Kamah na'ah t'nuvat hasadeh zo _____ .*
*Barukh hamakom sheb'ra'ah.*

How good is this (name of food).
Blessed is God who created it.[16]

Before eating add:

*For fruit that grows on trees . . .*

בָּרוּךְ אַתָּה יְיָ אֱלֹהֵינוּ מֶלֶךְ הָעוֹלָם בּוֹרֵא פְּרִי הָעֵץ.
*Barukh atah Adonai Eloheinu melekh ha'olam,*
*borei p'ri ha'etz.*

Blessed is God, for creating fruit of the trees.

*For produce that grows from the soil . . .*

בָּרוּךְ אַתָּה יְיָ אֱלֹהֵינוּ מֶלֶךְ הָעוֹלָם
בּוֹרֵא פְּרִי הָאֲדָמָה.
*Barukh atah Adonai Eloheinu melekh ha'olam,*
*borei p'ri ha'adamah.*

Blessed is God, for creating produce from the
earth.

**Upon eating cake or pastry made from grain grown in**
Eretz Yisrael, **say:**

בָּרוּךְ אַתָּה יְיָ אֱלֹהֵינוּ מֶלֶךְ הָעוֹלָם
בּוֹרֵא מִינֵי מְזוֹנוֹת.
*Barukh atah Adonai Eloheinu melekh ha'olam,*
*borei minei m'zonot.*

Blessed is God for creating varieties of grain.

**Upon eating a meal at the kibbutz, say:**

בָּרוּךְ אַתָּה יְיָ אֱלֹהֵינוּ מֶלֶךְ הָעוֹלָם
אֲשֶׁר בָּרָא מַעֲדַנִים לְעַדֵּן בָּהֶם נֶפֶשׁ כָּל חַי.
בָּרוּךְ אַתָּה יְיָ עַל הָאָרֶץ וְעַל מַעֲדַנֶּיהָ.

*Barukh atah Adonai Eloheinu melekh ha'olam,*
*asher bara ma'adanim l'aden bahem nefesh*
*kol chai.*

*Barukh atah Adonai, al ha'aretz v'al ma'adane-*
*ha.*

Blessed is God for creating delightful food to give
pleasure to living creatures.

Blessed is God for the land and its delights.[17]

Before eating bread, add:

How good is this bread. Blessed is God who created it.[18]

בָּרוּךְ אַתָּה יְיָ אֱלֹהֵינוּ מֶלֶךְ הָעוֹלָם
הַמּוֹצִיא לֶחֶם מִן הָאָרֶץ.

*Barukh atah Adonai Eloheinu melekh ha'olam,*
*hamotsi lechem min ha'aretz.*

Blessed is God, for bringing forth bread from the
earth.

After eating, say the following:

בָּרוּךְ אַתָּה, יְיָ אֱלֹהֵינוּ, מֶלֶךְ הָעוֹלָם, עַל הַגֶּפֶן
וְעַל פְּרִי הַגֶּפֶן, וְעַל תְּנוּבַת הַשָּׂדֶה, וְעַל אֶרֶץ
חֶמְדָּה טוֹבָה וּרְחָבָה שֶׁרָצִיתָ וְהִנְחַלְתָּ לַאֲבוֹתֵינוּ
לֶאֱכֹל מִפִּרְיָהּ וְלִשְׂבֹּעַ מִטּוּבָהּ. רַחֶם-נָא, יְיָ אֱלֹהֵינוּ,
עַל יִשְׂרָאֵל עַמֶּךָ, וְעַל יְרוּשָׁלַיִם עִירֶךָ, וְעַל צִיּוֹן
מִשְׁכַּן כְּבוֹדֶךָ. וּבְנֵה יְרוּשָׁלַיִם עִיר הַקֹּדֶשׁ בִּמְהֵרָה
בְיָמֵינוּ, וְהַעֲלֵנוּ לְתוֹכָהּ וְשַׂמְּחֵנוּ בְּבִנְיָנָהּ, וְנֹאכַל
מִפִּרְיָהּ וְנִשְׂבַּע מִטּוּבָהּ, וּנְבָרֶכְךָ עָלֶיהָ בִּקְדֻשָּׁה
וּבְטָהֳרָה. כִּי אַתָּה, יְיָ, טוֹב וּמֵטִיב לַכֹּל, וְנוֹדֶה לְּךָ
עַל הָאָרֶץ וְעַל פְּרִי הַגֶּפֶן. בָּרוּךְ אַתָּה, יְיָ, עַל הָאָרֶץ
וְעַל פְּרִי הַגֶּפֶן.

Blessed is God for the fruit of the vine and the produce of the field, for the lovely and spacious land that you gave to our ancestors, as a heritage from which to eat the produce and to be satisfied by its goodness. Have mercy, Eternal our God, on Israel your people, on Jerusalem your city, and on Zion, the abode of your glory. Rebuild the holy city of Jerusalem speedily and in our days. Bring us there and gladden us with its revival. May we eat of the fruit of the Land and enjoy its goodness—for which we praise you in holiness and purity. Because you are good and render good to all, we acknowledge you for the Land and for its produce.

בָּרוּךְ אַתָּה יְיָ הַטּוֹב וְהַמֵּטִיב.

Barukh atah Adonai hatov vehameitiv.

Blessed is God, who is good and does good.[19]

## For a Variety of Special Occasions

Israel is a land where our blessings were first formulated—and no wonder: there is so much that takes the breath away. The following list of blessings reflects the everyday wonders you may encounter. All the blessings are traditional, either taken directly from the *Siddur* or borrowed from rabbinic literature.

### On seeing a friend or relative whom you have not seen for over 30 days:

בָּרוּךְ אַתָּה יְיָ אֱלֹהֵינוּ מֶלֶךְ הָעוֹלָם
שֶׁהֶחֱיָנוּ וְקִיְּמָנוּ וְהִגִּיעָנוּ לַזְּמַן הַזֶּה.

Barukh atah Adonai Eloheinu melekh ha'olam, shehecheyanu v'ki'manu v'higiyanu laz'man hazeh.

Blessed is God who has kept us in life, sustained us and brought us to this moment.

***On seeing a friend or relative whom you have not seen for over a year:***

בָּרוּךְ אַתָּה יְיָ אֱלֹהֵינוּ מֶלֶךְ הָעוֹלָם מְחַיֵּה הַמֵּתִים.

*Barukh atah Adonai Eloheinu melekh ha'olam, m'chayeh hameitim.*

Blessed is God, who revives the dead.

***On seeing the wonders of nature: deserts, valleys, mountains, whatever moves you:***

בָּרוּךְ אַתָּה יְיָ אֱלֹהֵינוּ מֶלֶךְ הָעוֹלָם
עֹשֶׂה מַעֲשֵׂה בְרֵאשִׁית.

*Barukh atah Adonai Eloheinu melekh ha'olam, oseh ma'aseh v'reishit.*

Blessed is God, who shaped the work of creation.

***On seeing rain:***

בָּרוּךְ אַתָּה יְיָ אֱלֹהֵינוּ מֶלֶךְ הָעוֹלָם הַטוֹב וְהַמֵּטִיב.

*Barukh atah Adonai Eloheinu melekh ha'olam, hatov vehameitiv.*

Blessed is God who is good and does good.

***On seeing a rainbow:***

בָּרוּךְ אַתָּה יְיָ, אֱלֹהֵינוּ מֶלֶךְ הָעוֹלָם, זוֹכֵר הַבְּרִית
וְנֶאֱמָן בִּבְרִיתוֹ וְקַיָּם בְּמַאֲמָרוֹ.

*Barukh atah Adonai Eloheinu melekh ha'olam zokher habreet, v'ne'eman bivreeto v'kayam b'ma'amaro.*

Blessed is God who remembers the covenant, who is faithful to the covenant, and whose word stands firm.

*On hearing thunder, seeing lightning, or experiencing a violent windstorm:*

בָּרוּךְ אַתָּה יְיָ, אֱלֹהֵינוּ מֶלֶךְ הָעוֹלָם,
שֶׁכֹּחוֹ וּגְבוּרָתוֹ מָלֵא עוֹלָם.

*Barukh atah Adonai Eloheinu melekh ha'olam,
shekocho ug'vurato malei olam.*

Blessed is God whose might and power fill the universe.

*On seeing blossoming trees or shrubs:*

בָּרוּךְ אַתָּה יְיָ, אֱלֹהֵינוּ מֶלֶךְ הָעוֹלָם,
שֶׁלֹּא חִסַּר בְּעוֹלָמוֹ דָּבָר
וּבָרָא בוֹ בְּרִיּוֹת טוֹבוֹת וְאִילָנוֹת טוֹבִים
לְהַנּוֹת בָּהֶם בְּנֵי אָדָם.

*Barukh atah Adonai Eloheinu melekh ha'olam,
shelo chisar b'olamo davar uvara vo v'riyot
tovot v'ilanot tovim l'hanot bahem b'nei adam.*

Blessed is God whose universe lacks absolutely nothing, who has created it with beautiful creatures and lovely trees so that human beings may enjoy them.

*On seeing the new moon:*

בָּרוּךְ אַתָּה יְיָ אֱלֹהֵינוּ מֶלֶךְ הָעוֹלָם
מְחַדֵּשׁ רָאשֵׁי חֳדָשִׁים.

*Barukh atah Adonai Eloheinu melekh ha'olam,
m'chadesh roshei chodashim.*

Blessed is God, who renews the moon.

*On observing evidence of the love of the land among the people who live there:*

בָּרוּךְ אַתָּה יְיָ אֱלֹהֵינוּ מֶלֶךְ הָעוֹלָם
שֶׁנָּתַן חֵן מָקוֹם עַל יוֹשְׁבָיו.

*Barukh atah Adonai Eloheinu melekh ha'olam,
shenatan chen makom al yoshvav.*

Blessed is God, who inspires the inhabitants of a
place with love for where they dwell.

## On observing archeological remains of pagan worship:

בָּרוּךְ אַתָּה יְיָ אֱלֹהֵינוּ מֶלֶךְ הָעוֹלָם
שֶׁעָקַר עֲבוֹדָה זָרָה מֵאַרְצֵנוּ.

*Barukh atah Adonai Eloheinu melekh ha'olam,
she'akar avodah zarah me'artseinu.*

Blessed is God, who has uprooted idolatry from
our land.

## On seeing new homes for people who have resettled Israel's wasteland:

בָּרוּךְ אַתָּה יְיָ אֱלֹהֵינוּ מֶלֶךְ הָעוֹלָם
מַצִּיב גְּבוּל אַלְמָנָה.

*Barukh atah Adonai Eloheinu melekh ha'olam,
matsiv g'vul almanah.*

Blessed is God, who establishes landmarks for
the widowed country.

# For the Airplane: Prayer for a Safe Journey to Israel

מִי שֶׁבֵּרַךְ אֲבוֹתֵינוּ,
אַבְרָהָם יִצְחָק וְיַעֲקֹב,
שָׂרָה, רִבְקָה, רָחֵל וְלֵאָה,
יְבָרְכֵנִי
וְאֶת הַנּוֹסְעִים אִתִּי
בְּזוּ נְסִיעָתֵנוּ לְאֶרֶץ יִשְׂרָאֵל.
יְהִי רָצוֹן מִלְּפָנֶיךָ
שֶׁנִּסַּע לְשָׁלוֹם,
וְשֶׁנַּגִּיעַ בְּשָׁלוֹם לְאֶרֶץ חֶמְדַּת לִבֵּינוּ,

לְאֶרֶץ צִיּוֹן.
יְהִי רָצוֹן מִלְפָנֶיךָ שֶׁנַּחֲזֹר
מְבֹרָכִים בְּכָל מַעֲשֵׂינוּ,
מְחֻדָּשִׁים מֵעַמֵּנוּ בִּמְדִינָתֵנוּ.

God of our fathers and mothers,
Set us on our journey and guide us
that we may reach our destination joyously alive
    and at peace.
Deliver us from all danger on the way.
May we merit favor, kindness, and compassion in
    your sight,
and in the sight of all who see us.
Blessed are You, God, for hearing prayer.[20]

May the One who blessed our ancestors,
Abraham, Isaac and Jacob, Sarah, Rebekah, Rachel
    and Leah,
Bless me, _____ , and those who travel with me,
As we leave for the land of Israel.
May we travel there safely,
And arrive in peace to the land we hold dear,
the land we call Zion.
May we return, blessed in every undertaking,
Inspired and renewed by our people in our land.

## Meditation for Traveling to Israel: Am I a Tourist or a Pilgrim?

### Tourists, by Yehuda Amichai

Visits of condolence is all we get from them.
They squat at the Holocaust Memorial,
They put on grave faces at the Wailing Wall
And they laugh behind heavy curtains
In their hotels.
They have their pictures taken
Together with our famous dead
At Rachel's Tomb and Herzl's tomb
And on the top of Ammunition Hill.
They weep over our sweet boys
And lust over our tough girls

*And hang up their underwear*
*To dry quickly*
*in cool, blue bathrooms.*

Once I sat on the steps by a gate at David's
Tower. I placed my two heavy baskets at my side. A
group of tourists was standing around their guide
and I became their target marker.

"You see that man with the baskets? Just right of
his head there's an arch from the Roman period.
Just right of his head."

"But he's moving, he's moving!" I said to myself:
Redemption will come only if their guide tells them,
"You see that arch from the Roman period? It's not
important: but next to it, left and down a bit, there
sits a man who's bought fruit and vegetables for his
family."

## For the Airplane: Prayer for a Safe Journey Home

יְהִי רָצוֹן מִלְפָנֶיךָ, יְיָ אֱלֹהֵינוּ וֵאלֹהֵי אֲבוֹתֵינוּ,
שֶׁתּוֹלִיכֵנוּ לְשָׁלוֹם וְתַצְעִידֵנוּ לְשָׁלוֹם,
וְתַגִּיעֵנוּ אֶל מְחוֹז חֶפְצֵנוּ לְחַיִּים וּלְשִׂמְחָה וּלְשָׁלוֹם.
וְתַצִּילֵנוּ מִכַּף כָּל אוֹיֵב וְאוֹרֵב וְאָסוֹן בַּדֶּרֶךְ,
וְתִתְּנֵנוּ לְחֵן וּלְחֶסֶד וּלְרַחֲמִים
בְּעֵינֶיךָ וּבְעֵינֵי כָל רוֹאֵינוּ.
וְתִשְׁמַע קוֹל תַּחֲנוּנֵינוּ,
כִּי אֵל שׁוֹמֵעַ תְּפִלָּה וְתַחֲנוּן אָתָּה.
בָּרוּךְ אַתָּה, יְיָ, שׁוֹמֵעַ תְּפִלָּה.

*God of our fathers and mothers,*
*Set us on our journey and guide us*
*that we may reach our destination joyously alive*
    *and at peace.*
*Deliver us from all danger on the way.*
*May we merit favor, kindness, and compassion in*
    *your sight,*
*and in the sight of all who see us.*
*Blessed are You, God, for hearing prayer.*[21]

# On Waking Up and Going to Bed Each Day

## On Waking Up

בָּרוּךְ אַתָּה יְיָ אֱלֹהֵינוּ מֶלֶךְ הָעוֹלָם,
אֲשֶׁר יָצַר אֶת הָאָדָם בְּחָכְמָה,
וּבָרָא בוֹ נְקָבִים נְקָבִים, חֲלוּלִים חֲלוּלִים.
גָּלוּי וְיָדוּעַ לִפְנֵי כִסֵּא כְבוֹדֶךָ,
שֶׁאִם יִפָּתֵחַ אֶחָד מֵהֶם אוֹ יִסָּתֵם אֶחָד מֵהֶם
אִי אֶפְשָׁר לְהִתְקַיֵּם וְלַעֲמוֹד לְפָנֶיךָ.
בָּרוּךְ אַתָּה, יְיָ, רוֹפֵא כָל בָּשָׂר וּמַפְלִיא לַעֲשׂוֹת.

*We praise You, God,*
*for shaping humankind with wisdom,*
*for creating in us ducts and organs,*
*knowing well*
*that if this one opens or that one closes*
*our life on earth would end.*
*Blessed is God, whose work is marvelous.*

אֱלֹהַי, נְשָׁמָה שֶׁנָּתַתָּ בִּי טְהוֹרָה הִיא.
אַתָּה בְרָאתָהּ, אַתָּה יְצַרְתָּהּ, אַתָּה נְפַחְתָּהּ בִּי,
וְאַתָּה מְשַׁמְּרָהּ בְּקִרְבִּי, וְאַתָּה עָתִיד לִטְּלָהּ מִמֶּנִּי
וּלְהַחֲזִירָהּ בִּי לֶעָתִיד לָבֹא.
כָּל זְמַן שֶׁהַנְּשָׁמָה בְקִרְבִּי מוֹדֶה אֲנִי לְפָנֶיךָ,
יְיָ אֱלֹהַי וֵאלֹהֵי אֲבוֹתַי, רִבּוֹן כָּל הַמַּעֲשִׂים,
אֲדוֹן כָּל הַנְּשָׁמוֹת.
בָּרוּךְ אַתָּה, יְיָ, הַמַּחֲזִיר נְשָׁמוֹת לִפְגָרִים מֵתִים.

*My God, the soul You gave is pure.*
*You created it, shaped it, breathed it into me.*
*You care for it within me,*
*will some day take it from me,*
*and return it to me in a time to come.*
*As long as I have my soul, I will acknowledge You,*
*my God and God of those who came before me,*
*Master of material being and of the soul.*
*Blessed is God who restores souls to the dead.*

מוֹדֶה אֲנִי לְפָנֶיךָ, מֶלֶךְ חַי וְקַיָּם, שֶׁהֶחֱזַרְתָּ בִּי
נִשְׁמָתִי בְּחֶמְלָה; רַבָּה אֱמוּנָתֶךָ.

*Modeh ani l'fanekha melekh chai v'kayam*
*shehechezarta bi nishmati b'chemlah rabbah*
*emunatekhah.*

I give thanks to You, Eternal One,
For restoring my soul. Great is your faithfulness.[22]

## On Going to Bed

יְהִי רָצוֹן מִלְּפָנֶיךָ יְיָ אֱלֹהַי שֶׁתַּשְׁכִּיבֵנִי לְשָׁלוֹם
וְתֵן חֶלְקִי בְּתוֹרָתֶךָ
וְתַרְגִּילֵנִי לִידֵי מִצְוָה
וְאַל תַּרְגִּילֵנִי לִידֵי עֲבֵירָה
וְאַל תְּבִיאֵנִי לִידֵי חֵטְא וְלֹא לִידֵי עָוֹן וְלֹא לִידֵי
נִסָּיוֹן וְלֹא לִידֵי בִזָּיוֹן
וְיִשְׁלוֹט בִּי יֵצֶר טוֹב וְאַל יִשְׁלוֹט בִּי יֵצֶר הָרָע
וְתַצִּילֵנִי מִפֶּגַע רָע וּמֵחֳלָאִים רָעִים
וְאַל יְבַהֲלוּנִי חֲלוֹמוֹת רָעִים וְהִרְהוּרִים רָעִים
וּתְהֵא מִטָּתִי שְׁלֵמָה לְפָנֶיךָ
וְהָאֵר עֵינַי פֶּן אִישַׁן הַמָּוֶת
בָּרוּךְ אַתָּה יְיָ הַמֵּאִיר לָעוֹלָם כּוּלּוֹ בִּכְבוֹדוֹ.
בְּיָדוֹ אַפְקִיד רוּחִי בְּעֵת אִישַׁן וְאָעִירָה.
וְעִם רוּחִי גְּוִיָּתִי יְיָ לִי וְלֹא אִירָא.

*My God, lie me down in peace*
*and grant me a portion in your Torah.*
*Accustom me to mitzvot—*
*to doing good not evil.*
*Deliver me from sin and wrong,*
*from temptation and shame.*
*Let my inclination for good, not evil, reign me in.*
*Save me from mishap and disease;*
*let nightmares and nighttime thoughts not*
*    overwhelm me.*
*Let me sleep peacefully in your presence.*
*Wake me up, lest I sleep the sleep of the dead.*
*Blessed is God, who awakens the world with glory.*
*Asleep or awake, I leave my soul in God's hands.*
*And with my soul, my body too.*
*God is with me; I do not fear.[23]*

בָּרוּךְ אַתָּה יְיָ אֱלֹהֵינוּ מֶלֶךְ הָעוֹלָם
אֲשֶׁר קִדְּשָׁנוּ בְּמִצְוֹתָיו
וְצִוָּנוּ לְהַמְלִיכוֹ בְּלֵבָב שָׁלֵם,
וּלְיַחֲדוֹ בְּלֵב טוֹב,
וּלְעָבְדוֹ בְנֶפֶשׁ חֲפֵצָה.

*Barukh atah Adonai Eloheinu melekh ha'olam,*
*asher kidshanu b'mitzvotav*
*v'tsivanu l'hamlikho b'levav shalem*
*ul'yachado v'lev tov*
*ul'ovdo v'nefesh chafetsah*

Blessed is God,
who has sanctified us with commandments
and commanded us to recite the Sh'ma
to declare God's royalty with full intention,
to declare God's unity with good intent,
and to serve our God wholeheartedly.
Amen."[24]

שְׁמַע יִשְׂרָאֵל, יְיָ אֱלֹהֵינוּ, יְיָ אֶחָד.

*Sh'ma Yisrael Adonai Eloheinu Adonai Echad.*

Hear O Israel, Adonai is our God, Adonai alone.

# A Meal in Jerusalem

*or*

## How to Celebrate Like a Pilgrim

For Adonai your God brings you into a good
land, a land of brooks of water, of fountains
and depths that spring out of valleys and
hills; a land of wheat, and barley, and vines,
and fig trees, and pomegranates; a land of
olive oil, and honey; a land where you shall
eat bread without scarceness, you shall not
lack any thing in it; a land whose stones are
iron, and out of whose hills you may dig
bronze. When you have eaten and are full,
then you shall bless Adonai your God for the
good land which was given to you.

*—Deuteronomy 8:7–10*

## Before Eating

Psalm 126

שִׁיר הַמַּעֲלוֹת,
בְּשׁוּב יְיָ אֶת שִׁיבַת צִיּוֹן
הָיִינוּ כְּחֹלְמִים.
אָז יִמָּלֵא שְׂחוֹק פִּינוּ
וּלְשׁוֹנֵנוּ רִנָּה,
אָז יֹאמְרוּ בַגּוֹיִם
הִגְדִּיל יְיָ לַעֲשׂוֹת עִם אֵלֶּה.
הִגְדִּיל יְיָ לַעֲשׂוֹת עִמָּנוּ
הָיִינוּ שְׂמֵחִים.

*Shir hama'alot*
*B'shuv Adonai et shivat tsiyon*
*hayinu k'cholmim*
*Az yimalei s'chok pinu*
*Ul'shoneinu rinah*
*Az yomru vagoyim*
*Higdil Adonai la'asot im eleh*
*Higdil Adonai la'asot imanu*
*Hayinu s'meikhim*

When our God brought back those who returned
    to Zion,
We were like dreamers.
Our mouths were filled with laughter
Our tongues with shouts of joy.
Among the nations, people said,
"Adonai has done great things for these people."

Our God has done great things with us,
   and we rejoice.

בָּרוּךְ אַתָּה יְיָ אֱלֹהֵינוּ מֶלֶךְ הָעוֹלָם
הַמּוֹצִיא לֶחֶם מִן הָאָרֶץ.

*Barukh atah Adonai Eloheinu melekh ha'olam,*
*hamotsi lechem min ha'aretz.*

Blessed is God, who brings forth bread from the
earth.

## After Eating

To Redeem the Past
To Celebrate the Present
To Build the Future
A *Birkat Hamazon* from then to now.[1]

*These prayers we are about to say have not been*
*said for over 1,000 years.*

*Written by our people, here in our land, they*
*were recited for centuries, but died when our people*
*were chased from the land in the First Crusade*
*1,000 years ago. Recovered now, they are ours*
*again.*

*We make them our own in common identity with*
*our people through time, from the earliest expression*
*of their hopes to the present rebirth of the land*
*where those hopes were born.*

*We resurrect these prayers from the dust of cen-*
*turies, just as we have resurrected the dust itself to be*
*reborn as modern Israel.*

### INVITATION

(Leader:)

בִּרְשׁוּת רַבּוֹתַי, נְבָרֵךְ שֶׁאָכַלְנוּ מִשֶּׁלּוֹ.

Let us praise God of whose food we have eaten.

(Gathering:)

בָּרוּךְ שֶׁאָכַלְנוּ מִשֶּׁלּוֹ וּבְטוּבוֹ חָיִינוּ.

Praised be our God whose food we have eaten
and by whose goodness we live.

## BLESSING OF SUSTENANCE

(All:)

בָּרוּךְ אַתָּה, יְיָ, אֱלֹהֵינוּ מֶלֶךְ הָעוֹלָם,
הַזָּנִינוּ וְלֹא מִמַּעֲשֵׂינוּ,
הַמְפַרְנְסֵינוּ וְלֹא מִצִּדְקוֹתֵינוּ.
הַמַּעֲדִיף טוּבוֹ הַגָּדוֹל עָלֵינוּ, כָּאָמוּר:
"פּוֹתֵחַ אֶת יָדֶךָ וּמַשְׂבִּיעַ לְכָל חַי רָצוֹן."
מִטּוּבְךָ תַּשְׂבִּיעֵנוּ
כִּי אַתָּה יוֹצְרֵנוּ.
בָּרוּךְ אַתָּה, יְיָ, הַזָּן אֶת הַכֹּל.

Blessed are You, Adonai, our God, ruler of the
    universe,
For feeding us beyond the measure of our deeds,
And sustaining us beyond what we are worth.
You give us bountifully of your great goodness,
As it is written (Psalm 145:16):
    "You open your hand,
    satisfying the desire of every living thing."
Blessed are You, Adonai, for feeding all.

## BLESSING OF THE LAND OF ISRAEL

(All:)

עַל אַרְצֵינוּ וְעַל נַחֲלַת אֲבוֹתֵינוּ
נוֹדֶה לְךָ, יְיָ, אֱלֹהֵינוּ,
שֶׁהִנְחַלְתָּנוּ וְהִנְחַלְתָּ אֶת אֲבוֹתֵינוּ
אֶרֶץ חֶמְדָּה טוֹבָה וּרְחָבָה,
בְּרִית, וְתוֹרָה, וְחַיִּים וּמָזוֹן,
וְעַל שֶׁהוֹצֵאתָנוּ מִמִּצְרַיִם,
וּפְדִיתָנוּ מִבֵּית עֲבָדִים,

וְעַל תּוֹרָתְךָ שֶׁלִמַּדְתָּנוּ,

וְעַל הַכֹּל, יְיָ, אֱלֹהֵינוּ, אֲנַחְנוּ מוֹדִים לָךְ,

וּמְבָרְכִים אֶת שְׁמֶךָ.

יִתְבָּרַךְ שִׁמְךָ תָּמִיד לְעוֹלָם וָעֶד, כָּאָמוּר:

"וְאָכַלְתָּ וְשָׂבָעְתָּ וּבֵרַכְתָּ אֶת יְיָ אֱלֹהֶיךָ."

בָּרוּךְ אַתָּה, יְיָ עַל הָאָרֶץ וְעַל הַמָּזוֹן.

For our land, and our ancestral inheritance,
We thank You, Adonai, our God,
For bequeathing to us and to our ancestors
    A delightful, good and bountiful land,
    A covenant, Torah, life and food;
And for delivering us from Egypt
    and redeeming us from bondage;
And for the Torah that you taught us;
For everything, Adonai, our God,
    we thank You,
    and bless your name.
Let your name be blessed forever and ever,
As it is written (Deuteronomy 8:10):
    "When you eat and are satisfied,
    bless Adonai your God."
Blessed are You, Adonai, for the land and
    for its food.

## BLESSING OF JERUSALEM

(All:)

נַחֲמֵנוּ, יְיָ, אֱלֹהֵינוּ, בְּצִיּוֹן עִירֶךָ בְּרִנָּה,

וְרַחֵם, יְיָ, אֱלֹהֵינוּ,

עָלֵינוּ,

וְעַל יִשְׂרָאֵל עַמֶּךָ,

וְעַל יְרוּשָׁלַיִם עִירֶךָ,

וְעַל צִיּוֹן מִשְׁכַּן כְּבוֹדֶךָ,

וְעַל מַלְכוּת בֵּית דָּוִד מְשִׁיחֶךָ.

בִּמְהֵרָה תַּחֲזִירֶנָּה לִמְקוֹמָה, כִּי לְךָ, יְיָ,

מְיַחֲלוֹת עֵינֵינוּ.

וְתִבְנֶה צִיּוֹן עִיר קָדְשֶׁךָ, וְתִמְלוֹךְ עָלֵינוּ אַתָּה לְבַדֶּךָ,

וְתוֹשִׁיעֵנוּ לְמַעַן שְׁמֶךָ.

וְאַף עַל פִּי שֶׁאָכַלְנוּ וְשָׁתִינוּ,

חֻרְבַּן בֵּיתְךָ הַגָּדוֹל וְהַקָּדוֹשׁ לֹא שְׁכַחֲנוּ.
וְאַל תִּשְׁכָּחֵנוּ לָעַד
כִּי חָסִיד וְקָדוֹשׁ וּבָרוּךְ וְנֶאֱמָן אַתָּה, וְנֶאֱמָר:
"בּוֹנֵה יְרוּשָׁלַיִם יְיָ נִדְחֵי יִשְׂרָאֵל יְכַנֵּס."
בָּרוּךְ אַתָּה, יְיָ, הַבּוֹנֶה בְרַחֲמָיו אֶת יְרוּשָׁלָיִם.

Comfort us, Adonai, our God, in Zion, your city,
  With joy.
Have mercy, Adonai, our God,
    On us
    On Israel, your people,
    On Jerusalem, your city,
    On Zion, the dwelling place of your glory,
    And on the dominion of the house of David
      your messiah.
Quickly restore it to its place,
For we look only to You.
We have just eaten and drunk our fill,
But we have not forgotten the destruction
  of your great and holy house.
Do not ever forget it, yourself,
For You are pious, holy, blessed and faithful,
As it is written (Psalm 147:2),
"Adonai will build Jerusalem and restore
  the exiles of Israel."
Blessed are You, Adonai, for building Jerusalem
  in mercy.

## BLESSING OF GOOD TIDINGS

(All:)

בָּרוּךְ אַתָּה, יְיָ, אֱלֹהֵינוּ מֶלֶךְ הָעוֹלָם,
תִּתְבָּרַךְ לָעַד
הָאֵל אָבִינוּ, מַלְכֵּנוּ, מַחֲסֵינוּ, תּוֹחַלְתֵּינוּ,
  קְדוֹשֵׁינוּ, קְדוֹשׁ יַעֲקֹב.
רוֹעֵנוּ, וְרוֹעֵה יִשְׂרָאֵל,
הַמֶּלֶךְ הָרַחֲמָן, הַטּוֹב וְהַמֵּטִיב,
הָאֵל אֲשֶׁר בְּכָל יוֹם וָיוֹם
הוּא מַרְבֶּה לְהֵיטִיב לָנוּ.
הוּא גְמָלָנוּ,

הוּא גוֹמְלֵינוּ,
הוּא עָתִיד יִגְמְלֵינוּ לָעַד
חֵן וָחֶסֶד וְהַצְלָחָה וְכָל טוֹב.
הָרַחֲמָן יִמְלוֹךְ לְעוֹלָם וָעֶד.
הָרַחֲמָן יִתְעַלֶּה לְדוֹרֵי דוֹרִים.
הָרַחֲמָן קֶרֶן לְעַמּוֹ יָרִים.
הָרַחֲמָן יְחַיֵּינוּ וִיזַכֵּנוּ לִימוֹת הַמָּשִׁיחַ
וּלְחַיֵּי הָעוֹלָם הַבָּא.

Blessed are you, Adonai, our God, ruler of the
universe.
Be blessed forever,
Our God, parent and ruler,
Our protector and hope
Our holy One, the holy One of Jacob.
Our shepherd, the shepherd of Israel
Our merciful monarch,
who is good and does good
Our God who daily multiplies our good fortune.
You have rewarded us in the past,
You reward us even now,
You will reward us in the future,
with grace, compassion, success and
all good things.

May the all-merciful One reign forever.
May the all-merciful One be exalted for
all generations.
May the all-merciful One raise a horn of plenty
for our people.
May the all-merciful One grant us life, and
let us merit a messianic time and life in the
world to come.
Amen.

(It is customary here to pause long enough to allow anyone
who wishes to offer extemporaneous prayers, beginning
with, "May the all-merciful . . ." after which all assembled
answer, "Amen.")

May the all-merciful. . . . Amen.

## CONCLUSION

עֹשֶׂה שָׁלוֹם בִּמְרוֹמָיו, הוּא יַעֲשֶׂה שָׁלוֹם עָלֵינוּ
וְעַל כָּל יִשְׂרָאֵל, וְאִמְרוּ אָמֵן.

*Oseh shalom bimromav*
*Hu ya'aseh shalom aleinu*
*V'al kol yisra'el*
*V'imru amen.*

May the One who makes peace on high,
grant peace also to us, and to all Israel.
To which we say,
Amen.

# *Notes*

SECTION THREE
## *How to Shape Sacred Time*

1. Sometimes the book has endnotes, like this one. They are included to give you the chance to think through some of the spiritual insight behind the blessing. Do not stop to read endnotes while you are saying the blessing. But some time later, in your hotel room that night, perhaps, read the endnote with the blessing again. This will help you recollect the experience while it is still fresh in your memory. You will be able to reflect on a deeper understanding of what the blessing and the event may mean.

2. From the daily morning service; originally for a blessing for awakening to the dawn of a new day.

3. A reversal of the daily morning blessing *zokef kefufim,* "who raises up the fallen."

4. From the blessing that is traditionally said upon completing a journey safely.

5. From Jeremiah 33:10–11, a messianic promise of days to come.

6. From an ancient prayer used in the land of Israel; an old version of the *Amidah.*

7. From the service surrounding the Torah, but based on *Lamentations.*

SECTION FOUR
## *This Place Is Holy*

1. The various *aliyot* (waves of immigration) are divided as follows: First Aliyah (1882–1903), some 25,000 individuals and small groups, many of whom returned home in bitter failure. Second

Aliyah (1904–1914), largely from Russia, prompted to some extent by the Kishinev pogroms of 1903 and 1905, when the Czarist government supported wide-scale Jewish massacres, demonstrating to the Zionists that Jews should build up a Jewish homeland, above all else. Third Aliyah (1919–1923), again from eastern Europe, occasioned by the widespread destruction to Jewish communities devastated by World War I. Fourth Aliyah (1924–1928), mostly from Poland, and more urban than prior *aliyot,* a response to anti-Semitic outbreaks occasioned by the rise of post-war Polish nationalism. Fifth Aliyah (1929–1939), Jews fleeing the rise of Nazism. Some historians describe a Sixth and Seventh Aliyah also, referring those Jews who arrived during and after World War II. Certainly the recent arrival of Jews from Russia and Ethiopia are independent *aliyot* in their own right.

2. Frances Burnce, ed., *A. D. Gordon: Selected Essays* (Boston: Independent Press, 1938) and Simon Noveck, ed., *Contemporary Jewish Thought: A Reader* (Clinton, Mass.: Colonial Press, 1963).

3. Based on Jeremiah 31:19, "Ephraim is a dear son to me." The poet inserts Abraham for Ephraim and plays on his name, as well as that of the patriarch, Abraham, who follows God's command to "Go to the Land that I will show you." The passage in Jeremiah describes Ephraim (Joseph's son, and another name for Israel generally) as beloved to God; surely Abraham is also.

4. Based on Psalm 90:17, "Establish the work of our hands."

5. Ben-Zvi, Rachel Yanait, *Before Golda: Manya Shochat: A Biography,* Trans. Sandra Shurin. (New York: Biblio Press, 1989.)

6. Isaac Luria introduced liturgical meditations called *kavvanot,* in which he focused on the mystical intention behind the prayers. Our common notion of *tikkun olam* ("repairing the world"), though known to the Rabbis of antiquity, reemerged with Luria with the specific meaning of transforming the experience of fragmentation into perfect wholeness. In one way or another, that thought precedes all kabbalistic prayer and is also the ground for Chasidic spirituality.

7. From Lawrence Fine, *Safed Spirituality* (New York: Paulist Press, 1984).

8. The blessing appears first in the ancient Temple cult, from which it was taken over in the standard liturgy, where it appears several times. The introduction to the blessing is known as a *kavvanah.* Originally *kavvanah* meant "intention," paying attention to what was being said in prayer and not reciting words by rote. Kabbalistic thought converted the word into a technical term: the name for a meditation that precedes a mitzvah and draws our attention to its deeper mystical meaning. Believing that God is somehow

both male and female, they applied the term *Sh'khinah*, originally just a word for God's presence, to the feminine side of God. They believed that their performance of mitzvot served to reunite a divided deity into perfect harmony. Since the advanced notion of *kavvanah* had its origin at Safed, where above all, redemption was the focus of all prayers, the visit to Safed is accompanied by a prayer for redemption and the preceding *kavvanah*.

9. From the liturgy of Yom Kippur.

10. This translation of the Song of Songs is my own, but I have benefitted from Marcia Falk, *The Song of Songs: A New Translation (Love Lyrics from the Bible)* (New York: HarperSanFrancisco, 1993).

11. The traditional blessing from the daily *Amidah*, praying for agricultural abundance.

12. A play on words from Isaiah 40:3, which read, "A voice cries out, 'In the desert, clear a road . . .'" But it can be read, "A voice cries out in the desert: 'Clear a road . . .'" This blessing, new here, captures the sense of the work of restoring the desert to life as heeding a command heard here in the desert itself. It recollects also God's paradigmatic appearance to Moses at the burning bush and, at Sinai, to all of Israel—both of them desert experiences.

13. Israel T. Na'amani, David Rudavky, and Abraham I. Katch, eds., *Israel Through the Eyes of Its Leaders* (Tel Aviv: Meorot, 1971). I am also indebted to Michael Keren, *Ben-Gurion and the Intellectuals* (DeKalb, IL: Northern Illinois Press, 1983).

14. From an ancient prayer used in the land of Israel; an old version of the *Amidah*; applied here with reference to David Ben-Gurion.

15. The last two lines of the familiar liturgical poem *Adon Olam*, intended as a statement of faith in God even when we sleep our final sleep of death; followed by a traditional blessing affirming God's care for our people at all times.

16. Ronald Sanders, *The High Walls of Jerusalem* (New York: Holt, Rinehart and Winston, Inc., 1983).

17. A combination of the saying attributed to Rabbi Nachman of Bratslav and Psalm 118:5, both of which deal with strait places; followed by Psalm 126, which was recited by Chief Rabbi Hertz at the celebration by British Jews, following the announcement of the Balfour Declaration.

18. Adapted from the daily liturgy: the seventeenth benediction of the *Amidah*.

19. *Psalm 36: A Psalm Touching Genealogy.*

20. Psalm 135:21.

21. Raphael Patai, ed., Harry Zohn, trans., *The Complete Diaries of Theodor Herzl* (New York and London: Herzl Press & Thomas Yoseloff, 1960).

22. The traditional prayer recited upon visiting a grave.

23. Translation based on that which is provided by Cecil Roth, ed., *Encyclopedia Judaica*.

24. Illegal immigrants, generally smuggled past British border patrols.

25. Taken from the conclusion of the *Kaddish*.

26. Abraham Joshua Heschel, *Israel: An Echo of Eternity* (Woodstock, Vt.: Jewish Lights Publishing, 1997).

27. A prayer drawn from Abraham Joshua Heschel, and *Sha'arei Dim'ah*, a collection of traditional prayers for recitation at the Wall.

28. Based on the blessing for the pilgrimage festivals. The reference "rise up" points to the smoke of the sacrificial offering that prompted the prayer in the first place.

29. An ancient blessing attibuted by the Rabbis to the Temple's sacrificial cult. It was used regularly by Jews in Israel until the Crusades, and adopted anew by Reform Judaism's *Union Prayer Book*.

30. Gershom Scholem, *From Berlin to Jerusalem: Memories of My Youth* (New York: Schocken, 1980).

31. The traditional blessing to be said in the presence of a secular scholar.

32. From the standard morning prayers, recited when arising.

33. From the *Bet Ha-Shitah Kibbutz Haggadah,* 1947. The poem appears in Hebrew in Yosef Hayim Yerushalmi, *Haggadah and History* (Philadelphia: Jewish Publication Society, 1975). Translation here provided by Joel M. Hoffman.

34. *Yizkor* and *El Malei Rachamim*, the two prayers associated with memorializing the dead, and customary at all memorial services. The first was composed after the slaughter of Rhineland Jewry by the Crusaders in 1096; the second was written as a response to pogroms in the Ukraine in 1648. English versions are taken from *Gates of Repentance*, the High Holy Days prayer book of the Reform Movement.

35. From the daily morning liturgy.

36. From ancient fast day liturgy, when the Temple still stood.

37. Information drawn from Manfred Waserman and Amalie Moses Kass, "Moses Montefiore, a Hebrew Prayer Book, and Medicine in the Holy Land," *Judaism* 45 (1996): 324–32.

38. Borrowed from an insertion in the daily *Amidah*.

39. Psalm verses traditionally said to commemorate the death of Moses. These are normally said during to the Shabbat afternoon *(minchah)* synagogue service, because of the tradition that Moses died then. This translation is borrowed largely from *Siddur Sim Shalom*.

40. The traditional blessing for hearing news of a death, and for performing *k'riyah*, the ritual of cutting the ribbon or one's clothes at the funeral of immediate family members. Used also, by some, when lighting a *Yizkor* (memorial) lamp.

41. A combination of the traditional prayer customarily said in synagogue during the reading of the Torah, and the blessing assigned to the liturgy for the Sabbath that precedes each new month. Translations are based on those of *Siddur Sim Shalom*, the prayer book of the Conservative Movement.

42. The traditional blessing for seeing the Mediterranean.

43. From an ancient prayer from *Eretz Yisrael*, adopted by Italian Jewry, and then lost; recovered here for use in pilgrimages to the land where it was created.

44. From the *haftarah* blessings for Shabbat and an ancient blessing recited on fast days when the Temple still stood.

45. From a prayer first recorded in the ninth century, and customarily said to this day when people are called to the Torah.

46. From an ancient prayer on fast days, when the Temple still stood.

47. From the daily liturgy, the ninth benediction of the *Amidah*.


S E C T I O N   F I V E

## The Guide to Blessing

1. From the blessing preceding the morning recitation of the *Sh'ma* in the daily liturgy.

2. A combination of the traditional prayer for blessing, customarily said in a synagogue during the reading of the Torah, and the prayer for blessing assigned to the liturgy for the Shabbat that precedes each new month. Translations are based on those of *Sid-*

*dur Sim Shalom,* the prayer book of the Conservative movement.

3. From Talmud *Berakhot* 54a.

4. From the Siddur, a prayer associated with the act of Torah study.

5. Numbers 23:8; 20; 24:5.

6. The words for "sacred center" are biblical; they refer to the center of the ancient temple, the place that our ancestors believed was literally the axis of the world.

7. Format of the *Kaddish* with places interspersed is borrowed from *Siddur Sim Shalom,* the prayer book of the Conservative movement.

8. Translation is based on the version supplied in *Gates of Prayer,* the prayer book for the Reform movement.

9. The traditional blessing prescribed for standing in the presence of a Torah scholar; adapted here for recitation in places of wisdom.

10. The words of *Hatikvah* were written in 1878 by the poet Naftali Hertz Imber to celebrate the founding of the first Jewish settlement in Palestine, Petach Tikvah. In 1882, malaria had all but killed the first wave of settlers there, but Imber came to Israel and read the poem to farmers in nearby Rishon L'tsiyon. That very year, or shortly thereafter, Samuel Cohen, a recent immigrant who heard the poem, set it to music based on a Romanian folk melody. It was sung here and there, but became well known in 1905 when the Seventh Zionist Congress meeting in Basel ended with the song. In 1933 it was declared the Zionist national anthem.

At first, the last four lines read: "Our hope is not yet lost / The age-old hope / To return to the land of our fathers / To the city where David dwelt." With the founding of the state in 1948, the lyrics were changed to reflect the fact that the return had actually begun.

11. Blessing based on Jeremiah 17:13, "God is the hope of Israel."

12. A new blessing but based on the instructions in the Talmud to follow the interests of peace regarding relationships with non-Jews.

13. From the Midrash, *Avot d'Rabbi Natan* 2:31.

14. From the Talmud, *Ta'anit* 23a.

15. Based on a verse from the story of creation, Genesis 2:9.

16. From the Talmud, *Berakhot* 40b.

17. From the Palestinian Talmud, *Berakhot* 10:11.

18. From the Talmud, *Berakhot* 40b.

19. An ancient form of the *Birkat Hamazon* (Grace after Meals) intended especially for food that is grown in the land of Israel. We still recite it regularly at the Passover Seder. The reference to "who is good and does good" reflects the messianic hope implicit in every Jewish meal—that God may someday provide food for all. In keeping with that hope, a final line has been appended to the blessing here. The line occurs elsewhere independently as a blessing for hearing "good tidings" and therefore is messianic as well. It found its way into the traditional *Birkat Hamazon* also, so it is an appropriate conclusion.

20. English translation of *T'fillat Haderekh,* traditional prayer for a journey, from Talmud, *Berakhot* 29b. Hebrew is newly adapted by Joel M. Hoffman. For traditional Hebrew of *T'fillat Haderekh,* see p. 223.

21. *T'fillat Haderekh,* traditional prayer for a journey, from Talmud, *Berakhot* 29b.

22. Traditional prayers from the daily liturgy.

23. Prayers taken from Talmud, *Berakhot* 60b; and from traditional liturgy, the last two lines of *Adon Olam.*

24. An ancient blessing from *Eretz Yisrael* that we no longer say in our daily prayers, but is recovered here for use while visiting Israel.


## SECTION SIX

## *A Meal in Jerusalem*

1. The vitality of Jewish life in the land of Israel is particularly evident in its remarkable medieval prayer life. History proved kinder to Babylonian Jews, however; their worship service became the basis for what Jews do today, whereas Palestinian prayers were lost until the turn of the twentieth century. Only then did scholars discover a cache of manuscripts that included fragments of the prayers of Jews in *Eretz Yisrael.* This *Birkat Hamazon* is based on those manuscripts. It is a conglomerate assembled from the dazzling variety of compositions that typified Jewish life there prior to the Crusades.

*Birkat Hamazon* (Grace after Meals) is among our oldest prayers. It begins with an invitation, and is followed by four separate blessings thanking God for food in general, our land of Israel, Jerusalem, and good tidings to come—the messianic age. The entire set of prayers was probably messianic in that they thank God not just for what we already have, but for what we trust God will some day provide.

# Index of Places and Occasions for Which Prayers Are Provided

# About Jewish Lights

People of all faiths and backgrounds yearn for books that attract, engage, educate, and spiritually inspire.

Our principal goal is to stimulate thought and help all people learn about who the Jewish People are, where they come from, and what the future can be made to hold. While people of our diverse Jewish heritage are the primary audience, our books speak to people in the Christian world as well and will broaden their understanding of Judaism and the roots of their own faith.

We bring to you authors who are at the forefront of spiritual thought and experience. While each has something different to say, they all say it in a voice that you can hear.

Our books are designed to welcome you and then to engage, stimulate, and inspire. We judge our success not only by whether or not our books are beautiful and commercially successful, but by whether or not they make a difference in your life.

For your information and convenience, at the back of this book we have provided a list of other Jewish Lights books you might find interesting and useful. They cover all the categories of your life:

| | |
|---|---|
| Bar/Bat Mitzvah | Life Cycle |
| Bible Study / Midrash | Meditation |
| Children's Books | Parenting |
| Congregation Resources | Prayer |
| Current Events / History | Ritual / Sacred Practice |
| Ecology | Spirituality |
| Fiction: Mystery, Science Fiction | Theology / Philosophy |
| Grief / Healing | Travel |
| Holidays / Holy Days | Twelve Steps |
| Inspiration | Women's Interest |
| Kabbalah / Mysticism / Enneagram | |

Stuart M. Matlins, Publisher

*Or phone, fax, mail or e-mail to:*
**JEWISH LIGHTS Publishing**
Sunset Farm Offices, Route 4 • P.O. Box 237
Woodstock, Vermont 05091
Tel: (802) 457-4000 • Fax: (802) 457-4004 • www.jewishlights.com
*Credit card orders:* (800) 962-4544
(8:30AM–5:30PM ET Monday–Friday)
*Generous discounts on quantity orders. SATISFACTION GUARANTEED. Prices subject to change.*

**For more information about each book,
visit our website at www.jewishlights.com**

# Life Cycle
## Marriage / Parenting / Family / Aging

**Jewish Fathers:** A Legacy of Love
*Photographs by Lloyd Wolf. Essays by Paula Wolfson.*
*Foreword by Harold S. Kushner.*
Honors the role of contemporary Jewish fathers in America. Each father tells in his own words what it means to be a parent and Jewish, and what he learned from his own father. Insightful photos. 9½ x 9⅞, 144 pp with 100+ duotone photos, Hardcover, ISBN 1-58023-204-3 **$30.00**

**The Creative Jewish Wedding Book**
A Hands-On Guide to New & Old Traditions, Ceremonies & Celebrations
*By Gabrielle Kaplan-Mayer*
Provides the tools to create the most meaningful Jewish traditional or alternative wedding by using ritual elements to express your unique style and spirituality.
9 x 9, 288 pp, b/w photos, Quality PB, ISBN 1-58023-194-2 **$19.99**

**The New Jewish Baby Album**
Creating and Celebrating the Beginning of a Spiritual Life—
A Jewish Lights Companion
*By the Editors at Jewish Lights. Foreword by Anita Diamant.*
*Preface by Sandy Eisenberg Sasso.*
A spiritual keepsake that will be treasured for generations. More than just a memory book, *shows you how—and why it's important*—to create a Jewish home and a Jewish life. 8 x 10, 64 pp, Deluxe Padded Hardcover, Full-color illus., ISBN 1-58023-138-1 **$19.95**

**The Jewish Pregnancy Book**
A Resource for the Soul, Body & Mind during Pregnancy, Birth & the First Three Months
*By Sandy Falk, M.D., and Rabbi Daniel Judson, with Steven A. Rapp*
Includes medical information on fetal development, pre-natal testing and more, from a liberal Jewish perspective; prenatal *Aleph-Bet* yoga; and prayers and rituals for each stage of pregnancy. 7 x 10, 208 pp, Quality PB, b/w illus., ISBN 1-58023-178-0 **$16.95**

**Celebrating Your New Jewish Daughter:** Creating Jewish Ways to Welcome Baby Girls into the Covenant—New and Traditional Ceremonies *By Debra Nussbaum Cohen*
6 x 9, 272 pp, Quality PB, ISBN 1-58023-090-3 **$18.95**

**The New Jewish Baby Book, 2nd Edition:** Names, Ceremonies & Customs—A Guide for Today's Families *By Anita Diamant*
6 x 9, 320 pp, Quality PB, ISBN 1-58023-251-5 **$19.99**

**Parenting As a Spiritual Journey:** Deepening Ordinary and Extraordinary Events into Sacred Occasions *By Rabbi Nancy Fuchs-Kreimer* 6 x 9, 224 pp, Quality PB, ISBN 1-58023-016-4 **$16.95**

**Embracing the Covenant:** Converts to Judaism Talk About Why & How *Edited and with introductions by Rabbi Allan Berkowitz and Patti Moskovitz* 6 x 9, 192 pp, Quality PB, ISBN 1-879045-50-8 **$16.95**

**The Guide to Jewish Interfaith Family Life**
An InterfaithFamily.com Handbook *Edited by Ronnie Friedland and Edmund Case* 6 x 9, 384 pp, Quality PB, ISBN 1-58023-153-5 **$18.95**

**Introducing My Faith and My Community**
The Jewish Outreach Institute Guide for the Christian in a Jewish Interfaith Relationship *By Rabbi Kerry M. Olitzky*
6 x 9, 176 pp, Quality PB, ISBN 1-58023-192-6 **$16.99**

**Making a Successful Jewish Interfaith Marriage:** The Jewish Outreach Institute Guide to Opportunities, Challenges and Resources
*By Rabbi Kerry M. Olitzky with Joan Peterson Littman*
6 x 9, 176 pp, Quality PB, ISBN 1-58023-170-5 **$16.95**

**How to Be a Perfect Stranger, 3rd Edition:** The Essential Religious Etiquette Handbook
*Edited by Stuart M. Matlins and Arthur J. Magida*
The indispensable guide to the rituals and celebrations of the major religions and denominations in North America from the perspective of an interested guest of any other faith.
6 x 9, 432 pp, Quality PB, ISBN 1-893361-67-5 **$19.95** *(A SkyLight Paths book)*

# Spirituality

**The Alphabet of Paradise:** An A–Z of Spirituality for Everyday Life   *By Rabbi Howard Cooper*
Cooper spiritually illuminates the subjects of our daily lives—A to Z—examining these sources by using an ancient Jewish mystical method of interpretation that reveals both the literal and more allusive meanings of each.
5 x 7¾, 224 pp, Quality PB, ISBN 1-893361-80-2 **$16.95** *(A SkyLight Paths book)*

### Does the Soul Survive?: A Jewish Journey to Belief in Afterlife, Past Lives & Living with Purpose
*By Rabbi Elie Kaplan Spitz. Foreword by Brian L Weiss, M.D.*
Spitz relates his own experiences and those shared with him by people he has worked with as a rabbi, and shows us that belief in afterlife and past lives, so often approached with reluctance, is in fact true to Jewish tradition.
6 x 9, 288 pp, Quality PB, ISBN 1-58023-165-9 **$16.99**;
Hardcover, ISBN 1-58023-094-6 **$21.95**

### First Steps to a New Jewish Spirit: Reb Zalman's Guide to Recapturing the Intimacy & Ecstasy in Your Relationship with God
*By Rabbi Zalman M. Schachter-Shalomi with Donald Gropman*
An extraordinary spiritual handbook that restores psychic and physical vigor by introducing us to new models and alternative ways of practicing Judaism. Offers meditation and contemplation exercises for enriching the most important aspects of everyday life.   6 x 9, 144 pp, Quality PB, ISBN 1-58023-182-9 **$16.95**

### God in Our Relationships: Spirituality between People from the Teachings of Martin Buber
*By Rabbi Dennis S. Ross*
On the eightieth anniversary of Buber's classic work, we can discover new answers to critical issues in our lives. Inspiring examples from Ross's own life—as congregational rabbi, father, hospital chaplain, social worker, and husband—illustrate Buber's difficult-to-understand ideas about how we encounter God and each other.
5½ x 8½, 160 pp, Quality PB, ISBN 1-58023-147-0 **$16.95**

### The Jewish Lights Spirituality Handbook
A Guide to Understanding, Exploring & Living a Spiritual Life   *Edited by Stuart M. Matlins*
What exactly is "Jewish" about spirituality? How do I make it a part of my life? Fifty of today's foremost spiritual leaders share their ideas and experience with us.
6 x 9, 456 pp, Quality PB, ISBN 1-58023-093-8 **$19.99**;
Hardcover, ISBN 1-58023-100-4 **$24.95**

**Bringing the Psalms to Life:** How to Understand and Use the Book of Psalms   *By Dr. Daniel F. Polish*
6 x 9, 208 pp, Quality PB, ISBN 1-58023-157-8 **$16.95**;
Hardcover, ISBN 1-58023-077-6 **$21.95**

**God & the Big Bang:** Discovering Harmony between Science & Spirituality   *By Dr. Daniel C. Matt*
6 x 9, 216 pp, Quality PB, ISBN 1-879045-89-3 **$16.95**

**One God Clapping:** The Spiritual Path of a Zen Rabbi
*By Rabbi Alan Lew with Sherril Jaffe*
5½ x 8½, 336 pp, Quality PB, ISBN 1-58023-115-2 **$16.95**

**The Path of Blessing:** Experiencing the Energy and Abundance of the Divine   *By Rabbi Marcia Prager*
5½ x 8½, 240 pp, Quality PB, ISBN 1-58023-148-9 **$16.95**

**Six Jewish Spiritual Paths:** A Rationalist Looks at Spirituality   *By Rabbi Rifat Sonsino*
6 x 9, 208 pp, Quality PB, ISBN 1-58023-167-5 **$16.95**;
Hardcover, ISBN 1-58023-095-4 **$21.95**

**There Is No Messiah... and You're It:** The Stunning Transformation of Judaism's Most Provocative Idea   *By Rabbi Robert N. Levine, D.D.*   6 x 9, 192 pp, Quality PB, ISBN 1-58023-255-8 **$16.99**;
Hardcover, ISBN 1-58023-173-X **$21.95**

**These Are the Words:** A Vocabulary of Jewish Spiritual Life
*By Dr. Arthur Green*   6 x 9, 304 pp, Quality PB, ISBN 1-58023-107-1 **$18.95**

# Theology/Philosophy

**Aspects of Rabbinic Theology**
*By Solomon Schechter. New Introduction by Dr. Neil Gillman.*
6 x 9, 448 pp, Quality PB, ISBN 1-879045-24-9 **$19.95**

**Broken Tablets:** Restoring the Ten Commandments and
Ourselves *Edited by Rachel S. Mikva. Introduction by Lawrence Kushner.
Afterword by Arnold Jacob Wolf.*
6 x 9, 192 pp, Quality PB, ISBN 1-58023-158-6 **$16.95**;
Hardcover, ISBN 1-58023-066-0 **$21.95**

**Creating an Ethical Jewish Life**
A Practical Introduction to Classic Teachings on How to Be a
Jew
*By Dr. Byron L. Sherwin and Seymour J. Cohen*
6 x 9, 336 pp, Quality PB, ISBN 1-58023-114-4 **$19.95**

**The Death of Death**
Resurrection and Immortality in Jewish Thought
*By Dr. Neil Gillman*
6 x 9, 336 pp, Quality PB, ISBN 1-58023-081-4 **$18.95**

**Evolving Halakhah:** A Progressive Approach to Traditional
Jewish Law *By Rabbi Dr. Moshe Zemer*
6 x 9, 480 pp, Quality PB, ISBN 1-58023-127-6 **$29.95**;
Hardcover, ISBN 1-58023-002-4 **$40.00**

**Hasidic Tales:** Annotated & Explained
*By Rabbi Rami Shapiro*
*Foreword by Andrew Harvey, SkyLight Illuminations series editor*
5½ x 8¼, 240 pp, Quality PB, ISBN 1-893361-86-1 **$16.95**
*(A SkyLight Paths Book)*

**A Heart of Many Rooms**
Celebrating the Many Voices within Judaism
*By Dr. David Hartman*
6 x 9, 352 pp, Quality PB, ISBN 1-58023-156-X **$19.95**

**The Hebrew Prophets:** Selections Annotated & Explained
*Translation & Annotation by Rabbi Rami Shapiro*
*Foreword by Zalman M. Schachter-Shalomi*
5½ x 8¼, 224 pp, Quality PB, ISBN 1-59473-037-7 **$16.99**
*(A SkyLight Paths book)*

**Keeping Faith with the Psalms:** Deepen Your Relationship
with God Using the Book of Psalms *By Daniel F. Polish*
6 x 9, 272 pp, Hardcover, ISBN 1-58023-179-9 **$24.95**

**The Last Trial**
On the Legends and Lore of the Command to Abraham
to Offer Isaac as a Sacrifice
*By Shalom Spiegel. New Introduction by Judah Goldin.*
6 x 9, 208 pp, Quality PB, ISBN 1-879045-29-X **$18.95**

**A Living Covenant**
The Innovative Spirit in Traditional Judaism *By Dr. David Hartman*
6 x 9, 368 pp, Quality PB, ISBN 1-58023-011-3 **$18.95**

**Love and Terror in the God Encounter**
The Theological Legacy of Rabbi Joseph B. Soloveitchik
*By Dr. David Hartman*
6 x 9, 240 pp, Quality PB, ISBN 1-58023-176-4 **$19.95**;
Hardcover, ISBN 1-58023-112-8 **$25.00**

**Seeking the Path to Life**
Theological Meditations on God and the Nature of People,
Love, Life and Death *By Rabbi Ira F. Stone*
6 x 9, 160 pp, Quality PB, ISBN 1-879045-47-8 **$14.95**

**The Spirit of Renewal:** Finding Faith after the Holocaust
*By Rabbi Edward Feld*
6 x 9, 224 pp, Quality PB, ISBN 1-879045-40-0 **$16.95**

**Tormented Master:** *The Life and Spiritual Quest of Rabbi
Nahman of Bratslav By Dr. Arthur Green*
6 x 9, 416 pp, Quality PB, ISBN 1-879045-11-7 **$19.99**

**Your Word Is Fire:** The Hasidic Masters on Contemplative
Prayer *Edited and translated by Dr. Arthur Green and Barry W. Holtz*
6 x 9, 160 pp, Quality PB, ISBN 1-879045-25-7 **$15.95**

# Spirituality/Lawrence Kushner

## The Book of Letters
### A Mystical Hebrew Alphabet
Popular Hardcover Edition, 6 x 9, 80 pp, 2-color text,
ISBN 1-879045-00-1 **$24.95**
Deluxe Gift Edition with slipcase, 9 x 12, 80 pp, 4-color text,
Hardcover, ISBN 1-879045-01-X **$79.95**
Collector's Limited Edition, 9 x 12, 80 pp, gold foil embossed pages,
w/limited edition silkscreened print, ISBN 1-879045-04-4 **$349.00**

## The Book of Miracles
### A Young Person's Guide to Jewish Spiritual Awareness
*All-new illustrations by the author*
6 x 9, 96 pp, 2-color illus., Hardcover, ISBN 1-879045-78-8 **$16.95**
*For ages 9–13*

## The Book of Words: Talking Spiritual Life, Living Spiritual Talk
6 x 9, 160 pp, Quality PB, ISBN 1-58023-020-2 **$16.95**

## Eyes Remade for Wonder: A Lawrence Kushner Reader
*Introduction by Thomas Moore*
6 x 9, 240 pp, Quality PB, ISBN 1-58023-042-3 **$18.95;**
Hardcover, ISBN 1-58023-014-8 **$23.95**

## God Was in This Place & I, i Did Not Know
Finding Self, Spirituality and Ultimate Meaning
6 x 9, 192 pp, Quality PB, ISBN 1-879045-33-8 **$16.95**

## Honey from the Rock
An Introduction to Jewish Mysticism
6 x 9, 176 pp, Quality PB, ISBN 1-58023-073-3 **$16.95**

## Invisible Lines of Connection
Sacred Stories of the Ordinary
5½ x 8½, 160 pp, Quality PB, ISBN 1-879045-98-2 **$15.95**

## Jewish Spirituality—A Brief Introduction for Christians
5½ x 8½, 112 pp, Quality PB Original, ISBN 1-58023-150-0 **$12.95**

## The River of Light: Jewish Mystical Awareness
6 x 9, 192 pp, Quality PB, ISBN 1-58023-096-2 **$16.95**

## The Way Into Jewish Mystical Tradition
6 x 9, 224 pp, Quality PB, ISBN 1-58023-200-0 **$18.99;**
Hardcover, ISBN 1-58023-029-6 **$21.95**

# Ritual/Sacred Practice/ Journaling

## The Jewish Dream Book: The Key to Opening the Inner Meaning of Your Dreams *By Vanessa L. Ochs*
*with Elizabeth Ochs; Full-color illus. by Kristina Swarner*
Instructions for how modern people can perform ancient Jewish dream practices and dream interpretations drawn from the Jewish wisdom tradition. For anyone who wants to understand their dreams—and themselves.
8 x 8, 120 pp, Full-color illus., Deluxe PB w/flaps, ISBN 1-58023-132-2 **$16.95**

## The Jewish Journaling Book: How to Use Jewish Tradition to Write Your Life & Explore Your Soul
*By Janet Ruth Falon*
Details the history of Jewish journaling throughout biblical and modern times, and teaches specific journaling techniques to help you create and maintain a vital journal, from a Jewish perspective. 8 x 8, 304 pp, Deluxe PB w/flaps, ISBN 1-58023-203-5 **$18.99**

## The Rituals & Practices of a Jewish Life: A Handbook for Personal Spiritual Renewal *Edited by Rabbi Kerry M. Olitzky and Rabbi Daniel Judson*
6 x 9, 272 pp, illus., Quality PB, ISBN 1-58023-169-1 **$18.95**

## The Book of Jewish Sacred Practices: CLAL's Guide to Everyday & Holiday Rituals & Blessings *Edited by Rabbi Irwin Kula and Vanessa L. Ochs, Ph.D.*
6 x 9, 368 pp, Quality PB, ISBN 1-58023-152-7 **$18.95**

# Current Events/History

**The Story of the Jews:** A 4,000-Year Adventure—
A Graphic History Book
*Written & illustrated by Stan Mack*
Through witty, illustrated narrative, we visit all the major happenings from biblical times to the twenty-first century. Celebrates the major characters and events that have shaped the Jewish people and culture.
6 x 9, 288 pp, illus., Quality PB, ISBN 1-58023-155-1 **$16.95**

**The Jewish Prophet**
Visionary Words from Moses and Miriam to Henrietta Szold and A. J. Heschel
*By Rabbi Michael J. Shire*
6½ x 8½, 128 pp, Hardcover, ISBN 1-58023-168-3 **$14.95**

# Ecology

**Ecology & the Jewish Spirit**
Where Nature & the Sacred Meet   *Edited by Ellen Bernstein*
6 x 9, 288 pp, Quality PB, ISBN 1-58023-082-2 **$16.95**

**Torah of the Earth**
Exploring 4,000 Years of Ecology in Jewish Thought
Vol. 1: Biblical Israel: One Land, One People;
    Rabbinic Judaism: One People, Many Lands
Vol. 2: Zionism: One Land, Two Peoples;
    Eco-Judaism: One Earth, Many Peoples
*Edited by Rabbi Arthur Waskow*
Vol. 1: 6 x 9, 272 pp, Quality PB, ISBN 1-58023-086-5 **$19.95**
Vol. 2: 6 x 9, 336 pp, Quality PB, ISBN 1-58023-087-3 **$19.95**

# Spirituality/Prayer

**Pray Tell:** A Hadassah Guide to Jewish Prayer
*By Rabbi Jules Harlow, with contributions from Tamara Cohen, Rochelle Furstenberg, Rabbi Daniel Gordis, Leora Tanenbaum, and many others*
A guide to traditional Jewish prayer enriched with insight and wisdom from a broad variety of viewpoints—from Orthodox, Conservative, Reform, and Reconstructionist Judaism to New Age and feminist.
8½ x 11, 400 pp, Quality PB, ISBN 1-58023-163-2 **$29.95**

**My People's Prayer Book Series**
Traditional Prayers, Modern Commentaries
*Edited by Rabbi Lawrence A. Hoffman*
Provides diverse and exciting commentary to the traditional liturgy, helping modern men and women find new wisdom in Jewish prayer, and bring liturgy into their lives. Each book includes Hebrew text, modern translation, and commentaries from all perspectives of the Jewish world.
Vol. 1—The *Sh'ma* and Its Blessings
  7 x 10, 168 pp, Hardcover, ISBN 1-879045-79-6 **$23.95**
Vol. 2—The *Amidah*
  7 x 10, 240 pp, Hardcover, ISBN 1-879045-80-X **$24.95**
Vol. 3—*P'sukei D'zimrah* (Morning Psalms)
  7 x 10, 240 pp, Hardcover, ISBN 1-879045-81-8 **$24.95**
Vol. 4—*Seder K'riat Hatorah* (The Torah Service)
  7 x 10, 264 pp, Hardcover, ISBN 1-879045-82-6 **$23.95**
Vol. 5—*Birkhot Hashachar* (Morning Blessings)
  7 x 10, 240 pp, Hardcover, ISBN 1-879045-83-4 **$24.95**
Vol. 6—*Tachanun* and Concluding Prayers
  7 x 10, 240 pp, Hardcover, ISBN 1-879045-84-2 **$24.95**
Vol. 7—Shabbat at Home
  7 x 10, 240 pp, Hardcover, ISBN 1-879045-85-0 **$24.95**
Vol. 8—*Kabbalat Shabbat* (Welcoming Shabbat in the Synagogue)
  7 x 10, 240 pp, Hardcover, ISBN 1-58023-121-7 **$24.99**
Vol. 9—Welcoming the Night: *Minchah* and *Ma'ariv* (Afternoon and Evening Prayer)  7 x 10, 240 pp (est), Hardcover, ISBN 1-58023-262-0 **$24.99**  Avail. Nov. '05

# Holidays/Holy Days

## Reclaiming Judaism as a Spiritual Practice
Holy Days and Shabbat  *By Rabbi Goldie Milgram*
Provides a framework for understanding the powerful and often unexplained intellectual, emotional, and spiritual tools that are essential for a lively, relevant, and fulfilling Jewish spiritual practice.
7 x 9, 272 pp, Quality PB, ISBN 1-58023-205-1 **$19.99**

## 7th Heaven: Celebrating Shabbat with Rebbe Nachman of Breslov
*By Moshe Mykoff with the Breslov Research Institute*
Based on the teachings of Rebbe Nachman of Breslov. Explores the art of consciously observing Shabbat and understanding in-depth many of the day's traditional spiritual practices.
5⅛ x 8¼, 224 pp, Deluxe PB w/flaps, ISBN 1-58023-175-6 **$18.95**

## Creating Lively Passover Seders: A Sourcebook of
Engaging Tales, Texts & Activities  *By David Arnow, Ph.D.*
7 x 9, 416 pp, Quality PB, ISBN 1-58023-184-5 **$24.99**

## Hanukkah, 2nd Edition: The Family Guide to Spiritual
Celebration  *By Dr. Ron Wolfson. Edited by Joel Lurie Grishaver.*
7 x 9, 240 pp, illus., Quality PB, ISBN 1-58023-122-5 **$18.95**

## The Jewish Family Fun Book: Holiday Projects, Everyday
Activities, and Travel Ideas with Jewish Themes
*By Danielle Dardashti and Roni Sarig. Illus. by Avi Katz.*
6 x 9, 288 pp, 70+ b/w illus. & diagrams, Quality PB,
ISBN 1-58023-171-3 **$18.95**

## The Jewish Gardening Cookbook: Growing Plants &
Cooking for Holidays & Festivals  *By Michael Brown*
6 x 9, 224 pp, 30+ illus., Quality PB, ISBN 1-58023-116-0 **$16.95**

## The Jewish Lights Book of Fun Classroom Activities
Simple and Seasonal Projects for Teachers and Students
*By Danielle Dardashti and Roni Sarig*
6 x 9, 240 pp, Quality PB, ISBN 1–58023–206–X **$19.99**

## Passover, 2nd Edition: The Family Guide to Spiritual
Celebration  *By Dr. Ron Wolfson with Joel Lurie Grishaver*
7 x 9, 352 pp, Quality PB, ISBN 1-58023-174-8 **$19.95**

## Shabbat, 2nd Edition: The Family Guide to Preparing for and
Celebrating the Sabbath  *By Dr. Ron Wolfson*
7 x 9, 320 pp, illus., Quality PB, ISBN 1-58023-164-0 **$19.95**

**Sharing Blessings:** Children's Stories for Exploring the Spirit of the Jewish Holidays  *By Rahel Musleah and Michael Klayman*  8½ x 11, 64 pp, Full-color illus., Hardcover, ISBN 1-879045-71-0 **$18.95**  *For ages 6 & up*

# Spirituality/The Way Into... Series

*The Way Into...* Series offers an accessible and highly usable "guided tour" of the Jewish faith, people, history and beliefs—in total, an introduction to Judaism that will enable you to understand and interact with the sacred texts of the Jewish tradition. Each volume is written by a leading contemporary scholar and teacher, and explores one key aspect of Judaism. *The Way Into...* enables all readers to achieve a real sense of Jewish cultural literacy through guided study.

## The Way Into Encountering God in Judaism  *By Neil Gillman*
6 x 9, 240 pp, Quality PB, ISBN 1-58023-199-3 **$18.99**;
Hardcover, ISBN 1-58023-025-3 **$21.95**
Also Available: **The Jewish Approach to God: A Brief Introduction for Christians**  *By Neil Gillman*
5½ x 8½, 192 pp, Quality PB, ISBN 1-58023-190-X **$16.95**

## The Way Into Jewish Mystical Tradition  *By Lawrence Kushner*
6 x 9, 224 pp, Quality PB, ISBN 1-58023-200-0 **$18.99**;
Hardcover, ISBN 1-58023-029-6 **$21.95**

## The Way Into Jewish Prayer  *By Lawrence A. Hoffman*
6 x 9, 224 pp, Quality PB, ISBN 1-58023-201-9 **$18.99**;
Hardcover, ISBN 1-58023-027-X **$21.95**

## The Way Into Torah  *By Norman J. Cohen*
6 x 9, 176 pp, Quality PB, ISBN 1-58023-198-5 **$16.99**;
Hardcover, ISBN 1-58023-028-8 **$21.95**

# Spirituality/Women's Interest

### The Quotable Jewish Woman: Wisdom, Inspiration & Humor from the Mind & Heart
*Edited and compiled by Elaine Bernstein Partnow*
The definitive collection of ideas, reflections, humor, and wit of over 300 Jewish women.
6 x 9, 496 pp, Hardcover, ISBN 1-58023-193-4 **$29.99**

### The Women's Passover Companion
Women's Reflections on the Festival of Freedom
*Edited by Rabbi Sharon Cohen Anisfeld, Tara Mohr, and Catherine Spector*
Groundbreaking. A provocative conversation about women's relationships to Passover as well as the roots and meanings of women's seders.
6 x 9, 352 pp, Hardcover, ISBN 1-58023-128-4 **$24.95**

### The Women's Seder Sourcebook
Rituals & Readings for Use at the Passover Seder
*Edited by Rabbi Sharon Cohen Anisfeld, Tara Mohr, and Catherine Spector*
Gathers the voices of more than one hundred women in readings, personal and creative reflections, commentaries, blessings, and ritual suggestions that can be incorporated into your Passover celebration as supplements to or substitutes for traditional passages of the haggadah.
6 x 9, 384 pp, Hardcover, ISBN 1-58023-136-5 **$24.95**

**Lifecycles, Vol. 1:** Jewish Women on Life Passages & Personal Milestones *Edited and with introductions by Rabbi Debra Orenstein*
6 x 9, 480 pp, Quality PB, ISBN 1-58023-018-0 **$19.95**

**Lifecycles, Vol. 2:** Jewish Women on Biblical Themes in Contemporary Life *Edited and with introductions by Rabbi Debra Orenstein and Rabbi Jane Rachel Litman*
6 x 9, 464 pp, Quality PB, ISBN 1-58023-019-9 **$19.95**

**Moonbeams:** A Hadassah Rosh Hodesh Guide
*Edited by Carol Diament, Ph.D.*
8½ x 11, 240 pp, Quality PB, ISBN 1-58023-099-7 **$20.00**

**ReVisions:** Seeing Torah through a Feminist Lens
*By Rabbi Elyse Goldstein*
5½ x 8½, 224 pp, Quality PB, ISBN 1-58023-117-9 **$16.95**

**White Fire:** A Portrait of Women Spiritual Leaders in America
*By Rabbi Malka Drucker. Photographs by Gay Block.*
7 x 10, 320 pp, 30+ b/w photos, Hardcover, ISBN 1-893361-64-0 **$24.95** *(A SkyLight Paths book)*

**Women of the Wall:** Claiming Sacred Ground at Judaism's Holy Site *Edited by Phyllis Chesler and Rivka Haut*
6 x 9, 496 pp, b/w photos, Hardcover, ISBN 1-58023-161-6 **$34.95**

**The Women's Haftarah Commentary:** New Insights from Women Rabbis on the 54 Weekly Haftarah Portions, the 5 Megillot & Special Shabbatot *Edited by Rabbi Elyse Goldstein*
6 x 9, 560 pp, Hardcover, ISBN 1-58023-133-0 **$39.99**

**The Women's Torah Commentary:** New Insights from Women Rabbis on the 54 Weekly Torah Portions
*Edited by Rabbi Elyse Goldstein*
6 x 9, 496 pp, Hardcover, ISBN 1-58023-076-8 **$34.95**

**The Year Mom Got Religion:** One Woman's Midlife Journey into Judaism
*By Lee Meyerhoff Hendler* 6 x 9, 208 pp, Quality PB, ISBN 1-58023-070-9 **$15.95**

# Abraham Joshua Heschel

### The Earth Is the Lord's
The Inner World of the Jew in Eastern Europe
5½ x 8, 128 pp, Quality PB, ISBN 1-879045-42-7 **$14.95**

**Israel:** An Echo of Eternity *New Introduction by Susannah Heschel*
5½ x 8, 272 pp, Quality PB, ISBN 1-879045-70-2 **$19.95**

**A Passion for Truth:** Despair and Hope in Hasidism
5½ x 8, 352 pp, Quality PB, ISBN 1-879045-41-9 **$18.99**